MOUNTAIN MEDICINE
and
PHYSIOLOGY

PLAS Y BRENIN   FEBRUARY 1975

(Left) Michael Ward, Jack Longland, H.W. Tilman, John Jackson, Noel Odell, Charles Houston (Right)

MOUNTAIN MEDICINE
and
PHYSIOLOGY

*Proceedings of a Symposium
held by the Alpine Club at the
National Mountaineering Centre
Plas Y Brenin, Capel Curig,
North Wales,
26th – 28th February, 1975.*

Edited by
Charles Clarke
Michael Ward
Edward Williams

ALPINE CLUB
74 South Audley Street, London, W.1.

SBN 900523 17 4

Reprinted by arrangement with Alpine Club by
Mountain Safety Research, Inc.
631 South 96th Street
Seattle, Washington 98108   USA

2nd Printing August 1977

Mountain Safety Research has other books available and an excellent
selection of mountaineering and backpacking equipment. Send for
catalog.

Printed in Great Britain by R & C Moore & Co., 29 Barnsbury Square, London, N.1.
Typesetting on IBM Composer by Mason & Weldon Ltd., London, W.C.1.

Contents

The Chairmen at the meeting were John Jackson, Ron James, Dr. Charles Warren and Sir Jack Longland.

Foreword

This symposium, arranged by the Alpine Club, was the first of its kind, and it attracted over sixty interested people to Plas y Brenin, the National Mountaineering Centre, in February, 1975. They included distinguished physicians and surgeons, experts in mountain physiology, equipment, nutrition, hypoxia, hypothermia, oedema, frostbite and haemorrhoids, together with mountaineers, instructors and guides whose mountain experience covered most of the mountain ranges of the world. I do not think that, in this particular field, there has been a comparable assemblage of theoretical and practical knowledge, with a strong emphasis on the latter, and it was the unanimous wish of those who attended that abstracts of the papers and talks which we listened to at Plas y Brenin, together with very brief notes of the often passionate discussions which followed them, should be made available to those who are concerned with, and may be personally affected by the problems which we considered during a very full two-and-a-bit days. And we were all glad to hear that, through Dr. Charles Houston, a somewhat similar conference will take place in the Yosemite this autumn, and that Michael Ward who, with Edward Williams, was primarily responsible for instigating our Plas y Brenin symposium, will be representing British mountaineering and British medicine there.

To the non-medical mountaineer the most salutary result of the symposium was that the well established treatments were exposed as dangerous and possibly lethal mishandlings, and that much that had been transmitted to today's climbers by their founding fathers was grotesquely wrong. We had been taught to jolly, and if need be, frog-march youngsters suffering from hypothermia or exposure rapidly downhill and there are few surer ways of killing them. Frostbitten fingers were to be vigorously rubbed, preferably with snow, now stigmatised as a form of 'violent therapy', certain to do more harm than good. Nor were the surgeons much in advance in their knowledge: "Probably many unnecessary amputations have been carried on because of impatience at the very slow recovery". And we had come to regard mountain sickness, hypoxia, as a necessary, tiresome but essentially harmless concomitant of climbing to high altitudes. Perhaps we were so entranced by the exploits, without an oxygen set, at and above 8000 metres, of our uniquely endowed old friend Professor Odell, that we forgot to notice that others fared ill, and some never came home at all.

To me the most convincingly pungent conclusions of the symposium came from Dr. Drummond Rennie, reinforced by observations made by Michael Ward and others. High altitude climbers face an only recently recognised killer, oedema, either in its more frequent pulmonary or in its less common cerebral form, and both are inextricably associated with mountain sickness. In earlier Everest expeditions, in studies of miners working too high among the Andes, in aviation history, we had plenty of clues, but were not skilled at unravelling them.

Let Drummond Rennie speak, in that forthright style which endeared him to the Plas y Brenin symposium. "The two extreme manifestations of Acute Mountain Sickness kill people, and because these are people who go up into the mountains, they kill the young, the fit, the enthusiastic, the audacious and the hard working, and they are killing them in ever increasing numbers, . . . Shortage of oxygen is always a potentially dangerous condition, it can paralyse, render unconscious, stop the breathing and kill."

The fully documented warnings of Dr. Rennie and others who spoke at the symposium are not likely to discourage climbers who wish to test themselves in arctic or high altitude conditions. But they will leave them with less excuse for foolishly disregarding the now known results of operating over fairly long periods in such conditions. Even in the competitive climbing world of today, there is still something to be said for the highly skilled guide who remarked: "I don't want to be the best climber, I want to be the oldest climber." And if he pays heed to the scientific knowledge, research and practical experience of those who spoke at the Plas y Brenin symposium on Mountain Medicine and Physiology, he will have a reasonable chance of reaching his goal.

JACK LONGLAND,
President, Alpine Club.

Everest Without Oxygen

MICHAEL WARD

Evidence from mountaineers who have climbed to between 27,000 ft and 28,000 ft suggests that this represents the highest altitude attainable without oxygen. One mountaineer described this experience as like a sick man walking in a dream; another recorded hallucinations, and it is probable that two men have died as a direct result of their hypoxic state.

However some mountaineers have considered that they turned back at those great altitudes on the North side of Everest more as a result of bad climatic conditions than due to their own debility.

The example, too, of one man, Professor N. E. Odell who, in 1924, twice climbed without oxygen to above 27,000 ft and who spent eleven days above 21,000 ft does suggest that there may be exceptional individuals who could climb to the top of Mount Everest without the use of oxygen.

A number of people, using supplementary oxygen have reached the summit of Everest. Some have stayed at best for up to two hours without oxygen. One Sherpa has been twice to the top of Everest, and on the last occasion spent one hour without oxygen before symptoms developed. In addition four acclimatized American mountaineers having ascended Everest by two different routes bivouacked at about 28,500 ft without oxygen. Two were severely frostbitten; the other two were unscathed.

Climbing at great altitudes imposes two main stresses, those of high altitude and of cold. The stress of high altitude depends on the partial pressure of oxygen in the air, and the effectiveness of acclimatisation could be said to depend partly on the efficiency with which the fall in pressure of oxygen from the air to the tissues is minimized, and partly on changes occurring at tissue and cellular level.

The accompanying table shows the partial pressure of oxygen (pO_2) in mm Hg at varying stages in the oxygen transport system at sea-level and 29,000 ft.

	Ambient (Environmental)	Alveolar (Lung)	Arterial	Mixed Venous
Sea Level	150	100	95	45
Top of Everest (29,000 ft)	?45	? 24-31	?20	?12

These figures show that at the top of Everest, whilst at rest, the ambient pO_2 is roughly equivalent to the venous pO_2 at sea-level.

Under experimental conditions an acclimatized visitor has been kept at 30,000 ft (Alveolar pO_2 = 31 mm Hg) for thirty minutes, and at 32,000 ft (Alveolar pO_2 = 24 mm Hg) for a short period, without loss of consciousness.

It is usually accepted that cells can function at an intra-cellular pO_2 of 1—5 mm Hg. It can be seen therefore that at 29,000 ft this level may be attained at rest. (The mixed venous pO_2 is approximately equal to the cellular pO_2). During exercise however when oxygen is used up more rapidly and the pO_2 falls, the intra-cellular pO_2 may well fall below the critical level. Because the cells of the cerebral cortex are those most sensitive to oxygen lack, the mental features of hypoxia, including fixity of purpose and poor judgement, are the first to appear.

As the ambient pO_2 varies from day to day according to local climatic conditions, and as there is also a variation according to latitude and season then there will be periods when at 29,000 ft the ambient pO_2 will be higher (but the physical altitude will remain the same) and this will provide a higher driving force for oxygen, and thus the intra-cellular pO_2 will be higher.

Individuals also show varying abilities to work at high altitude and this will depend to some extent on the effective use of their oxygen transport system. The high altitude native is more efficient in this respect than the sea-level visitor and is capable of a higher work output at altitude, as shown by several instances on pre-war expeditions when Sherpas carried relatively immense loads without oxygen to great altitude.

The least understood mechanism of adaptation to hypoxia is that occuring at cellular level and it may well be the most important. An increase in myoglobin, mitochondria, tissue capillaries and changes in enzyme systems have been reported. These changes probably explain why individuals who have on many occasions been to high altitude adapt faster and better than newcomers. Individual variation is considerable and predictions about performance and acclimatisation are often inaccurate.

Other clinical features must also be taken into account. Above a critical altitude of 17,500 ft the phenomenon of high altitude deterioration occurs.

4

Mental and physical deterioration accelerates both with increasing altitude and with increasing length of stay. The main features are increasing weight loss associated with a poor appetite, and non-recovery from fatigue. Laboratory studies suggest that muscle glycogen re-synthesis may be impaired as also may intestinal absorption of certain carbohydrates.

Edocrine changes, as yet not fully understood are also likely to be of some importance. Fluid intake may also be greatly diminished at altitude. This is due partly to the blunting of the sensation of thirst. In addition fluid replacement depends on melting snow and facilities may be inadequate due to weather and living conditions. Considerable fluid loss from the lungs (up to 1500 ml/day) may occur as a result of increased respiration. Urine output appears to approach the minimal obligatory volume in all mountaineers who have been to altitudes exceeding 26,000 ft without oxygen.

The second main stress of climbing at great heights is cold. The temperature falls 3°F for every 1000 ft, and on the top of Everest the highest temperature must always be around or below freezing point. An additional factor is the wind which both lowers the effective temperature on an exposed surface (wind-chill effect) and is an extra factor in the production of muscular fatigue.

To stay in temperature balance the mountaineer must be adequately insulated and his food, fluid and oxygen intake must be satisfactory. Whilst insulation by clothing is now so effective that heat adaptation has been recorded whilst wearing polar clothing, bulky clothes increase oxygen consumption both due to their weight and to the effect of friction during movement. Heat production may be inefficient at altitude as food and fluid intake and oxygen consumption are inadequate and heat loss from the lungs is increased as a result of excessive respiration. Thus heat balance is disturbed.

A mountaineer may then be in a position where despite being fully clothed he is unable to maintain his normal core temperature (37°C). Initially cooling of the peripheral tissue to the environmental temperatures, which are usually below freezing, will occur. This inevitably results in frostbite. The central core temperature now falls. At about 33°C he will undergo uncontrollable shivering attacks comparable to rigors, and then becomes unconscious. If he is not warmed his central core temperature will fall still further and death from ventricular fibrillation will occur. This chain of events is reversed by heat, oxygen, food and fluid.

In summary it is probably possible for an adequately acclimatized person to work at 29,000 ft for short periods in a decompression chamber. To attain the summit of Mount Everest with the added hazards of the mountain environment in addition to those of hypoxia and cold may be possible but it would be a risky procedure.

Essentially an individual would need both the desire and the physiological ability. A life spent at high altitude provides a "Sherpa" physiology — most Sherpas, however, would probably find no adequate reason for wishing to climb

Everest without oxygen. The sea-level mountaineer may for his own reasons wish to try this feat but does not have the physiological ability.

It is natural for man to wish to stand on the highest point on earth by his own unaided efforts, and I have no doubt this will be attempted, but a support group alongside using oxygen would be a prudent safeguard.

Physiology of the Response to Low Temperature

R. E. MOORE

Man is a homeotherm, which means that he attempts to maintain a constant deep body temperature. The 'deep body' or 'core' is, at its minimum size, the heart, lungs, brain and liver, whilst the remainder of the body, that is the surface layers, limbs and lower belly, constitutes the 'shell'. The core and shell concept is very useful, for one can visualize the core expanding into the shell in the heat and retreating again in the cold. This is the major part of the 'heat stored' item in the following equation:

$$\text{Heat produced} = \text{heat lost} \pm \text{heat stored.}$$

When the constancy of the core temperature is threatened, physiological mechanisms are invoked to resist the change, these being autonomic and behavioural. Whereas all animals exhibit behavioural thermoregulation to a greater or lesser extent, it is only birds and mammals which have both. The information that a threat exists comes from temperature sensors in the skin and in the brain, and appropriate action is taken to avert or minimize a change in core temperature. A number of situations exist in which core temperature changes naturally, for example there is a 24 hour cycle of rise and fall but in this article these are ignored.

In considering the 'heat stored' item in the equation, it must be realised that this is essentially a short term device which allows a temporary imbalance to occur between heat production and heat loss. The situation which the body prefers is one in which core temperature is about $37.0^{\circ}C$ and skin temperature about $32.0^{\circ}C$, this giving the shell room for manoeuvre in both directions.

Heat Production

Heat is produced continuously as a result of metabolic processes, even when we are completely at rest. Three different aspects can be distinguished:

(a) Basal
(b) Thermoregulatory
(c) Exercise

7

Basal heat production arises from essential minimal processes of life, and is usually thought of as a fixed rate which can only be altered slowly and thus is of little use in defending against a sudden cold threat. It is partly controlled by the thyroid gland and in theory this fact could be exploited in the treatment of overt or incipient hypothermia.*

Thermoregulatory heat production is the end product of deliberately wasteful metabolism, a process with no other useful function than rapidly to produce heat. In the adult it is brought about mostly by shivering, a muscular contraction sequence which starts off as an increase in the tone or resting tension of opposing muscle groups. Initially this makes the limb feel stiff to move and impedes fine control of movement, and it develops into rapid oscillatory movements in which the muscle groups pull on their opposing muscles across a joint and cause reflex contractions of increasing violence. Although heat production increases to as much as three times basal, one's purposive movements and behavioural responses are impaired. There is another mechanism available to the infant which utilizes the enormous metabolic capacity of a special sort of fat known as brown adipose tissue. In the adult this and other non-shivering mechanisms would only account for about 10% of the total thermoregulatory heat production.

Exercise clearly and obviously produces heat as a by-product. In fact only a very small fraction of our muscular effort is usefully converted to external work, and the remainder, anything between 75% and 100%, turns up as body heat. In a short burst of maximal effort, heat production can rise to ten times basal for say ten minutes in a fit young man; it might rise to five times basal for an hour or two in a more sustained but less violent effort.

In the real life situation, exercise consists of purposive movements, and the heat produced will be dissipated by the body's heat losing mechanisms. As far as the body is concerned heat is heat no matter where it comes from, and therefore thermoregulatory heat production in the cold will be reduced if exercise is taken. However, in an acutely chilled fit person — where core temperature has fallen by say 1°C, exercise will not suppress the violent shivering, for the simple reason that it is the fall in temperature which is the stimulus, and until core temperature is raised to near normal, shivering will continue.

Heat production can be interfered with in a variety of ways which can be grouped under three heads:–

(a)   Failure of the breathing system adequately to control blood gases.

(b)   Failure of the circulation adequately to perfuse active tissues.

(c)   Failure of the nervous system to appreciate, activate and control events.

Climbers at high altitude are aware of the risks of hypoxia, in which the low oxygen pressure is responsible for poor oxygenation of the blood. Any mechanical block of the air tubes, infection of the lungs, or any condition which renders

*see paper by E.S.Williams.

8

breathing painful, exacerbates this and causes an additional restriction on the delivery of oxygen to the blood. Low blood oxygen pressure in its turn restricts the delivery of oxygen to tissues making it difficult for active muscle to maintain a high metabolic rate. It also inhibits nerve cell activity which has repercussions on behaviour as well as the control of shivering and non-shivering heat production (see below).

Circulation of the blood must be maintained in order to deliver oxygen and fuels to and remove products of metabolism from all tissues, but especially brain, heart and active muscles. If the heart does not pump effectively, tissues become hypoxic for the blood is the vehicle by means of which oxygen and other substances are transported. The circulation may fail because of blood loss or water loss through diarrhoea and vomiting, or because the heart itself is short of oxygen, or because the return of venous blood to the heart is reduced as in shock. One may sweat during severe exercise and fail to replace the water and salts and thus deplete the body fluids.

The central nervous system is essential for overall control of body functions. Information comes in from sense organs and the brain and spinal cord must accept the information, process it and regulate the effector mechanisms accordingly. Thus muscle contractions must be coordinated and controlled to produce movements which are meaningful at each moment in time. The best compromises must continually be found between purposive movements, maintenance of posture and balance, shivering, in which huge numbers of muscle fibres are made to contract and relax to just the correct degree, sequence and frequency to optimize one's chances of survival in its broadest sense. These immensely complex processes involve millions of nerve cells and must be at all times exquisitely sensitive to changing circumstances. It is little wonder therefore that anything which interferes with nerve cell function be it hypoxia or glucose lack, alcohol or other drugs with tranquillizing, anaesthetic or soporific actions, fatigue (whatever that is), or sleeplessness, are all likely to reduce the brain's ability to call forth thermoregulatory heat in a cold-threat situation.

Heat Loss

The physical laws governing heat loss apply as much to man as to an inanimate object: man however can exercise some control of the situation. The four processes are

    (a)   conduction,
    (b)   convection,
    (c)   radiation,
    (d)   evaporation,

and all can work to transfer heat to or from the body.

Conduction, or the transfer of heat by direct contact is most important in water immersion where heat loss may be so rapid that survival can be measured in minutes even in temperate waters unless the man is wearing proper insulative clothing. Air is a poor conductor and so therefore is dry clothing. Sodden clothing loses much of its insulative value.

Convection is the carrying away of heat by 'particles' of air or water which have been heated up during contact with the body by a process of conduction. The nude body at rest in still air is surrounded by a layer of warm air, which being less dense than colder air gently rises in the form of natural convection currents. The layer may be several centimetres thick, and is an effective blanket in still air conditions, but it is disrupted readily by even a light breeze. Windproof clothing curtails this stripping process and thus reduces heat loss from the covered areas. It is important to realise that a thin layer of impervious material next to the skin may be of virtually no insulative value: conduction will readily occur across the 0.1 mm thickness of commonly available polythene sheet and convection will then occur outside it. To be of real value it should be on the outside of a poorly conducting layer e.g. woollen garment, where it will prevent the wind stripping the insulating air cells of the clothing.

Radiation is the process of transfer of energy by non-particulate means. Light, ultra violet, radio waves and infrared (or heat) are all the same fundamentally; the difference is merely a matter of wave length. Heat loss can be serious on clear nights where the exposed surface is interacting with very cold outer space. Radiant loss is proportional to the fourth power of the temperature of the surface and the body gains from as well as loses to its surroundings. Direct sunshine through the dust free atmosphere at high altitude can add considerable heat to the body.

Evaporation of water is accompanied by cooling to the extent of about 0.6 Kcal/G. Normally about 500 ml daily are evaporated into the respired air and across the skin by diffusion, and anything from zero to ten or more litres per day is secreted by sweat glands: the latter is a thermoregulatory response, controlled by the brain. A man who is exercising in the cold may sweat, and the liquid sweat absorbed into clothing will continue to evaporate after the need for body cooling is over, and this can add considerably to the cold stress. Wetting by rain has the same effect, i.e. enforced cooling, with a need for the body to metabolize more fuel to generate additional heat.

Sensing Mechanisms

Temperature sensors are found in the skin and in the core. Those in the skin are part of the body's early warning system whereas those in the core are mainly located in that part of the brain known as the hypothalamus. The two types work in concert, but skin sensors are probably more important in rating comfort and in behavioural responses, whereas the deep sensors are very sensitive and probably affect shivering, sweating and other autonomic responses to a greater degree.

Thermally Induced Behaviour

If a man feels cold he does something about it. His responses are such as to bring the conditions next to the skin — the microclimate — to minimal thermal stress, and if possible economise on shivering or sweating which use up fuel or water reserves. Therefore he seeks shelter, puts on more clothing, builds a fire, or huddles with his fellows. He will adjust his behaviour to take account of other priorities, and will, for example, put himself at risk by rushing out into the cold inadequately clad in the interests of speed to rescue a fellow man or gather fuel. Accurate judgement allows a mouse to live in a cold store and briefly move out of his insulated nest to forage for food. But the penalty for misjudgement will be hypothermia, collapse and death if either fails to return to base in time.

The Metabolic Response to Cold

The Figure shows diagramatically the way that heat production varies in response to cold stress — here defined simply in terms of environmental air temperature (T_{air}). For a nude man at rest in still air, heat production is basal in the range 28–33°C T_{air}, the so called Thermoneutral zone. If T_{air} is lowered then heat production must rise if core temperature is to be defended, and the slope of the line indicates the efficiency of the man's subcutaneous fat as an insulator.

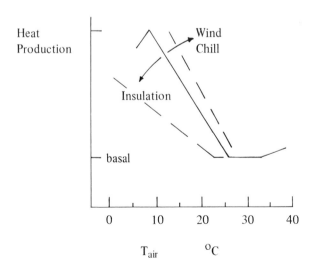

The relationship of heat production to environment temperature in a nude man at rest in still air is shown by the solid line. Heat production is at its lowest or basal rate in the comfortably warm range 28–33°C (approx.) As environmental temperature falls, heat production is increased by shivering and other means to maintain thermal balance.

The effect of wind (upper broken line) is to increase cold stress, the stronger the wind the steeper the line must be.

The effect of clothing and other insulation (lower broken line) is to reduce cold stress. The more insulation the shallower the line will be.

Maximal heat production (non-exercising) is about three times basal, but exercise can raise it by a factor of about five for sustained exercise and up to ten or even more for short periods in a trained athlete.

Cold stress may be increased or decreased in various ways. The Figure shows two broken lines flanking the solid one. The upper shows the relationship that would hold if cold stress was increased for example by wind chill and the lower one if it were decreased for example by increasing insulation. Thus, maximal heat production might be achieved at T_{air} 15°C in the former, but only on dropping T_{air} to say −10°C in the latter. It is therefore of prime importance, when judging the stressful nature of the environment, to remember that many factors must be considered: the following list gives the most important. It is convenient to assume that T_{air} is fixed at + 10°C for the purposes of comparison.

Factors which affect cold stress

Increase	Decrease
Wind	Insulation
Wetting	Huddling
Exhaustion	Shelter
Injury	Solar radiation
Drugs	Exercise
Hypoxia	

Note: *Stress* is imposed on the body causing a *strain* to be set up within the body.

Most of these have been mentioned already, but a few words on exhaustion and huddling are necessary. Exhaustion implies that fuel supplies — glucose in particular have run low, and that muscle end-products of metabolism have accumulated. We recognise also mental exhaustion although we cannot define it physiologically; the same applies to leadership quality and the will to survive, and there is no doubt that injury exacerbates exhaustion and reduces survival potential. A group of apparently identically fit people will not all become exhausted together.

Huddling is the standard behavioural response of many animals to cold stress; it causes an effective increase in body size, and therefore a relative decrease in body surface exposed. Children are at greater risk then adults in the cold because of their greater surface area : weight ratio.

Hypothermia

If the core temperature falls below $35^{\circ}C$ ($95^{\circ}F$), the implications are that the body has been stressed beyond its ability to maintain thermal equilibrium and active measures are required to rewarm it. Treatment must be careful, for two main reasons. First there will be exhaustion of glucose supplies and the muscles will be unable to contract properly. Secondly, the body shell consisting of up to half the body weight will be at an average temperature of perhaps $20^{\circ}C$ or less than the core. Any measures which cause the warm central blood to flow through the cold shell will cause the core temperature to fall even further. With the probable exception of rapid-onset immersion hypothermia, it is doubtful if *rapid* rewarming in the adult has any advantages.

The Deep Domestic Bath Treatment for Advanced Cases of Hypothermia

L. W. DAVIES

It is far better to put the patient fully clothed, even though soaking wet, straight into the sleeping bag or bath, rather than waste time pulling wet anoraks and pullovers off him. Usually when a patient is suffering from exposure he is in the fetal, curled up, position and time wasted in trying to straighten him out to remove his clothing could prove fatal.

Deep Bath Treatment

It is important to use the right technique. The water should NEVER be allowed to be as low as normal body temperature. Once water at $98.4^{\circ}F$ or lower surrounds the patient his reserve of body heat will then start to warm the water and death may occur as core temperature falls.

The bath water should be between $113^{\circ}F$ and $122^{\circ}F$ ($45^{\circ}C$ and $50^{\circ}C$).

The reason for these figures is that a severely hypothermic fully clothed cold wet human adult placed in a bath can cause the bath water temperature to be reduced by up to $12.6^{\circ}F$ within a few seconds. The environmental temperature of the air and the sides of the bath itself can rapidly bring this temperature down a further four to five degrees so that if, at the outset, the water is below $113^{\circ}F$ the patient can soon find himself in water below body heat. It is most important that the water in the bath should be constantly stirred to obviate the danger of a layer of water next to his body becoming colder than the rest of the water in the bath.

The only exceptions to the above water temperature should be in the case of frostbite when the affected parts should be held out of the water until the temperature has reduced to $108^{\circ}F$. In the case of children or where a heart condition is suspected, or in obese persons, $108^{\circ}F$ is the recommended maximum temperature.

Once sweat appears on the brow of the patient he can be removed from the bath but it is essential that he is kept in a horizontal position with his head

14

slightly lower than his feet. On no account should his buttocks or hips be allowed to sag as he is lifted out of the bath.

Whilst the patient is being warmed in the bath a bed should be prepared. The bed should have its sheets and pillow removed and be previously warmed, either by an electric blanket or by a healthy human being stripped to his underwear. The patient, still wet, is transported to the bed in a warm blanket.

The foot of the bed should be raised about ten inches by placing heavy books or other objects under the legs. The patient should be kept in the bed with his head covered as much as possible until medical help arrives. Normally he will sleep for several hours and there will then be a complete recovery. Warm sweet drinks should be given to him as soon as he is conscious and able to swallow them.

It cannot be emphasised too strongly that on no occasion should the patient be rubbed with towels or have hot water bottles placed near his body. *Unconscious patients are the ones that need the Deep Bath Treatment most.*

To immerse a man's hands in hot water whilst the remainder of his body is in an exposed state is likely to cause death because it would bring on the exchange of warm core blood with the colder blood at the periphery. The best method of warming, if still on the mountains, is to insulate the casualty from all further heat loss by placing him in a sleeping bag and to surround him with plastic and other forms of covering, the whole cocoon being further protected by being in a tent. At all times keep the head slightly below the body to facilitate blood flow to the brain.

Discussion

Prof. Moore considered that the hot bath treatment described by Sq. Ldr. Davies could be highly dangerous. A bath water temperature of 50°C would 'cook' the patient. Other speakers agreed.

Sq. Ldr. Davies explained that his hypothermic patients were fully clothed and soaked with cold water and that the water temperature on the skin was acceptably low.

Other speakers voiced misgivings in case 50°C became fixed in rescuers' minds, as the 'correct' bath water temperature and used it for treating a lightly clad or unclothed casualty. If the water temperature at the skin were this high the casualty would die.

Dr. Lloyd was sceptical of the hot bath treatment described but Sq. Ldr. Davies observed that a farmer in the Pennines had used his hot-bath treatment on fifty lambs and saved their lives.

Prof. Moore. For how long did they live?

Sq. Ldr. Davies. They themselves lambed successfully.

Prof. Moore. We do our tests on old people. Our treatment is nothing like as hot as that for Davies' people. We also find hypothermic patients on streets.

There is considerable local œdema at 43°–45° water temperature.

Sq. Ldr. Davies. Keeping the clothing on, which we do, undoubtedly does cool the water off very quickly. By far the most important thing to do is to keep the body temperature well above 98.4^oF. These chaps are often very nearly dead when we get them to a bath. A bath insufficiently hot causes harm not good.

Dr. F. Jackson. If the patient's temperature is below 90^oF you will be heating him with any heat which is above his body temperature. Sqn. Ldr. Davies' instructions, if interpreted literally, would cook people.

Dr. Nelms. I say Dr. Jackson is quite right. If you use the words '50^oC', then it is vital to say also 'because the water will cool down'.

Surgeon Commander Golden. Very hot temperatures are, historically, used for people who appear to be dead or nearly dead. The principle is to put more heat into the body. Classically the treatment was for seamen who had been cooled by water. In the fells exhaustion is a factor. Perhaps causing loss of thermo-regulating power. At the stage of great exhaustion I would seriously challenge the use of hot bath treatment.

Dr. Nicol. I have analysed all the fatalities particularised in the Scottish Mountaineering Club Journal since 1895 and would make the point that of those who died only two or three were alive at the time the Rescue Party arrived – in whatever shape or form it came. And furthermore, very few had been alive within the twelve hours preceding the arrival of the Rescue Party. That is, they were long dead. The message is clear: Prevention is better than cure.

Dr. Brotherhood. Hypothermia 'on the Hill'. An important question is *WHERE* are you going to treat it. Hot baths do not grow on hillsides. And it is very difficult to take a body off the hill. Can the patient be treated on the mountainside?

Reference was then made to sheep being rewarmed in experiments with polythene bags and it was thought that this could be done with humans. Speakers pointed out that when moving a hypothermic patient it is desirable to note that the circulation is very unstable. Pugh was quoted. He had noted that five out of twenty-three of his patients had convulsions when they were moved. Removal of clothes too is traumatic. *CUT* clothes off, and use a good pair of scissors. That is a good tip – to include an efficient pair of scissors in the First Aid Bag.

Sq. Lrd. Davies. Play down the idea of evacuation when on the mountain.

Airway Warming in Accidental Hypothermia

E. LL. LLOYD

In cold weather man is losing heat through the lungs with the heat loss as moisture being greater than heat loss as heat per se. For example, at an air temperature of $0^{\circ}C$ moisture loss accounts for 14.78 Kcal/hr out of a total respiratory heat loss of 20.94 Kcal/hr.

A hypothermic victim at $30^{\circ}C$ core temperature has a basal heat production reduced by 50% to about 60 Kcal/hr. Despite perfect body insulation he is still losing the 20.94 Kcal/hr through his lungs. Provision of heated humidified air to breathe abolishes this loss and instead of 40 Kcal/hr for rewarming the full 60 Kcal/hr is available — an increase of 50%. Any further heat or moisture supplied is a bonus.

In anaesthetised sheep, spontaneous rewarming with good surface insulation was estimated to require 11 hr 30 mins to reach normothermia. The addition of airway warming shortened this time to three hours (assisting the ventilation did not help the rate of warming). The hot bath required one hour to rewarm the sheep but, in the rescue situation, if transport to and the preparation of the bath are considered, the time for airway warming is very competitive.

The interaction of carbon dioxide and soda lime provides heat and moisture and by breathing through the soda lime this heat and moisture is transferred to the patient. This equipment, incorporating at least a container for soda lime and some form of replaceable or refillable cylinder for carbon dioxide, has been made portable and different versions have been used in the field on two occasions.

Dr Lloyd then gave a demonstration of his equipment which Mr Peter Bell had helped to construct.

References

Adams, J.M., and Goldsmith, R. (1965). 'Cold Climates' in 'Exploration Medicine'. Edholm, O.G. and Bacharach, A.L. Eds. pp 259. *John Wright & Sons Ltd., Bristol.*

Burton, A.C. and Edholm, O.G. (1955). 'Man in a Cold Environment'. Chaps 2 and 11. *Edward Arnold (Publishers) Ltd., London.*

Lloyd, E. LL., Conliffe, N.A., Orgel, H., and Walker, P.N. (1972). Accidental Hypothermia: an apparatus for Central Re-warming as a First Aid Measure. *Scottish Medical Journal 17,* 83–91.

Lloyd, E. LL. (1973). Accidental Hypothermia treated by Central Re-warming through the Airway. *British Journal of Anaesthesia, 45,* 41–48.

Lloyd, E.LL., and Frankland, J.C. (1974). Accidental Hypothermia: Central Re-warming in the Field. *British Medical Journal, 4,* 717.

Discussion

Dr. Warren described difficulties experienced with the Matthews respirator. It consisted of a small mask covering the nose and mouth. There were layers of gauze in a filter. His party had had to remove many of the layers of gauze because of the obstruction caused to breathing. If just a few layers were left it was more comfortable. It retained heat and was more moist. The soda-lime apparatus (closed apparatus) in which the oxygen was recirculated and passed through a soda canister, had had to be abandoned because of the heat which it generated.

Dr. Rennie said that L. R. G. C. Pugh asserted that one of the chief justifications for using oxygen apparatus was the conservation of heat.

Mr. Ward agreed. Those who used the closed apparatus in 1953 were much warmer. Had Dr. Lloyd used it, he asked.

Dr. Lloyd said that Bell had used it. It was possible to obtain total body insulation and let the subject breathe after putting a mask on.

Dr. Milledge sought information on Dr. Lloyd's recent work. Dr. Lloyd showed slides and demonstrated heat loss through the lungs at different temperatures. He described his experiments with sheep in polythene bags. The problem he said was not to produce heat so much as to control it.

Frostbite

MICHAEL WARD

Definition

Injury due to cold may be general or local. In general cold injury, or hypothermia, the individual is said to be suffering from exposure. Local cold injury may occur at temperatures above freezing (wet-cold conditions), as in immersion or trench foot. At temperatures below freezing (dry-cold conditions) frostbite occurs; the tissues freeze and ice crystals form in between the cells. Local cold injury may or may not be associated with hypothermia[1].

People at Risk

In civilian life frostbite is uncommon despite populations of about 100 million at risk in areas where sub-zero temperatures occur at some period of the year. During war at sub-zero temperatures frostbite is more common, often as a complication of wounds or disease. In the winter of 1943 frostbite injuries among U.S. heavy bomber crews were greater than all their other casualties combined[2].

Polar travellers of the pre-1920 era suffered severely and frostbite seems to have been common. More recently, increased knowledge and better equipment have lowered the incidence in polar regions, though among mountaineers at high altitude cases still occur regularly. Nevertheless, frostbite is not inevitable even at high altitude and the three highest of the world's peaks have been successfully climbed without cold injury.

Temperature Regulation

A useful but oversimplified concept is to imagine the body as consisting of a central core with a relatively uniform temperature of $37^{\circ}C$, and an insulating shell, with a temperature of $33^{\circ}C$. Heat transfer within the body occurs by convection through the circulation and by conduction through the peripheral tissue to the skin surface. As the maintenance of the central core temperature is

19

essential to life this may be carried out at the expense of the peripheral expendable structures such as the toes and fingers.

Normally mountaineers operate at about 60% of working capacity – thus at sea level, with a normal maximum oxygen intake of 3 l./min, they operate at 2 l./min. If for any reason this working capacity is lowered, they will have to work nearer maximum capacity to keep warm. If they are unable to keep up heat production, the periphery will cool to the ambient temperature (which may be below freezing point) and then the central core temperature will fall. At progressively higher altitudes the maximal oxygen consumption falls until at 24,500 ft (7,460 m) it is about 1·5 l./min[3]. At extreme altitudes the margin between maximum oxygen consumption and that necessary for work and heat production narrows, and cases of mild frostbite of the fingers and toes have been recorded in healthy well-clad people while climbing.

Heat loss from the body is prevented by the insulation of the tissues, air, and clothes. Of these, that provided by the clothes is the most important. Because of the greater relative surface area, the heat loss from the curved surface of a small cylinder is greater than that of a larger curved cylinder, and increasing the thickness of insulating material will not increase the total insulation greatly until a cylinder is more than about 1 in in diameter. As the normal finger is about 0.5–0.75 in (1.25–2.0 cm) in diameter, the fingers are difficult to insulate effectively even when a mitt glove is used.

Pathophysiology

Skin freezes when fingers have been immersed in brine at -1.9°C. The true freezing point, however, is about -0.53°C. The skin of the fingers can be cooled to temperatures below its true freezing point without freezing. Such "super cooling" is common if the skin is dry. On further cooling, freezing spreads rapidly in the super-cooled tissues, with tissue hardening.

Two main reactions take place when tissues come into contact with a very cold object. Firstly, a vascular reaction occurs under the frozen superficial tissues consisting of damage to the wall of the blood vessels, leakage of plasma into the tissues (forming blisters), and an increased viscosity of the remaining intra-vascular blood, with local haemoconcentration or "sludging". The small vessels may thus become blocked.[4] If the blood flow is then stopped by the action of the precapillary sphincters, the arteriovenous shunts will open up and blood bypasses the frozen area, which becomes avascular: in other words, the diseased part is sacrificed for survival of the whole organism. The second reaction is the form-ation of intercellular ice crystals. The intra-cellular osmotic pressure rises and enzyme mechanisms are disturbed with subsequent cell death.

Tissues vary in their resistance to frostbite. Skin appears to freeze at -0.53°C, while muscles, blood vessels, and nerves are also highly susceptible. Connective tissue, tendons, and bone are relatively resistant. Thus the blackened extremities of a frostbitten hand or foot can be moved since the tendons under the gangrenous skin remain intact, and the muscles to which these tendons belong are far removed from the area of severe cold injury.

High Altitude and Cold Injury

Frostbite at high altitude seems to be commoner for comparable conditions of cold than at lower levels. Both cold and high altitude raise the blood packed cell volume and viscosity and slow the peripheral blood flow. Cold injury to capillary walls leads to plasma leakage and intravascular sludging. This local haemoconcentration will be increased at altitude, and impaired tissue nutrition and necrosis may occur more rapidly.

Dehydration, the result of abnormal water loss from the lungs due to increased respiration, will also increase the viscosity of the blood, and thrombosis may be encouraged by relative inactivity over 21,000 ft. (6,400 m). Even at normal temperatures, the blood flow in the skin is reduced at high altitude, the result of arteriolar vasoconstriction.[5] Cardiac output is also decreased,[6] as may be basal metabolic rate. Moreover, the maximal oxygen uptake is progressively lowered with altitude, and with it the ability to increase heat production through exercise, and so is the ability to shiver. Hypoxia also blunts mental function and precautions normally taken against cold injury may be inadequate. Poor appetite – a cardinal feature of high altitude deterioration – may mean that calorie intake is inadequate with resulting diminution of the insulating layer of subcutaneous fat.

The only factor where high altitude does not appear to potentiate liability to cold injury is the wind-chill factor. Because of the relatively less dense atmosphere, this is diminished by comparison with sea-level values.

Clinical Features

Frostnip

Frostbite damages the tissues, whereas frostnip produces reversible changes. The skin blanches, and becomes numb with a sudden and complete cessation of cold and discomfort in the affected part. A tingling sensation may occur on rewarming. With immediate treatment frostnip will not progress to frostbite.

Superficial Frostbite

Only the skin and subcutaneous tissues immediately adjacent are concerned in superficial frostbite. The frozen part, though white and frozen on the surface, is soft and pliable when pressed gently before thawing. After rewarming, it becomes numb, mottled, blue or purple, and it will then sting, burn, or swell for a period.

Blisters may occur within 24—48 hours, depending on the site of the injury. Thus blistering is more common on the dorsum of the fingers and hand, where the tissues are lax, than on the palm. The blister fluid is slowly absorbed; the skin hardens and becomes black, producing a thick insensitive carapace of tissue. In certain sites the black carapace may occur without preceding blister formation.

There is associated oedema, and within weeks a very definite line of demarcation occurs. Throbbing or aching may persist for weeks. If the contour of the blackened carapace corresponds to that of the original part, then loss of tissue is unlikely. If, however, the contour of the pulp of the finger disappears, and the carapace has a tendency to wrinkle, then loss of tissue is likely.

Unlike that in arteriosclerosis, gangrene occurring after frostbite is essentially superficial, and the necrotic tissue may not extend more than a few millimetres in depth. The black carapace fits like a glove around the tissues and peels off bit by bit over the months. After the carapace has been shed, the underlying shiny red babyskin will be abnormally tender and unduly sensitive to heat and cold. Abnormal sweating may occur. In two or three months it will gradually take on the appearance of normal skin. Generally the subcutaneous tissue feels rather wooden for the same period, but gradually becomes more pliable. The nail may be lost but is likely to grow again either normally or with a wrinkled appearance.

Deep Frostbite

Deep frostbite involves not only the skin and subcutaneous tissue but also the deeper structures, including muscle, bone, and tendons. The affected part becomes cold, mottled, and blue or grey, and may remain swollen for months. Blistering may take weeks to develop but is not inevitable. Initially the part may be painless, but shooting and throbbing pains may occur and frequently abnormal sensations are encountered for up to two months.

As tendons are resistant to cold injury, the patient will be able to move his fingers and toes for long periods despite their gangrenous appearance. Thus even with severe frostbite patients can walk and use their fingers and hands for crude movements such as gripping. Eventually, a carapace forms and sloughs off. Often a complete cast of the finger or toe with nail attached may separate.

Permanent loss of tissue is almost inevitable with deep frostbite, and this may be surmised from the shrivelled appearance of the affected finger or toe. Even with a diagnosis of deep frostbite, however, a limb may return almost to normal over some months, and amputation should never be carried out until a considerable period (probably at least six to nine months) has elapsed.

Treatment

Prevention

It is extremely important to dress for the temperature with which the part will be in contact. In deep powder snow, the feet can be in snow many degrees below freezing point, while at the same time the ambient temperature may be many degrees above freezing. Even the ambient temperature may vary enormously, with a 50°C drop at sunset.

Principles

FROSTNIP

Frostnip is the only form of frostbite that should be treated on the spot. As this commonly occurs on the exposed portions of the body, such as the cheek or nose, each person should keep a watch for these signs in other members of the party. As soon as whitening of the skin is observed it is treated immediately. A place sheltered from the wind is found, or the back is turned to the wind, and the affected part is warmed by the hand, or the glove. Once the normal colour and consistency of the area is obtained normal working is resumed.

FROSTBITE

For many years rubbing the affected part, either with snow or with the normal hand, has been advocated for treating frostbite. This method neither melts the intercellular ice crystals by raising the temperature nor increases the blood supply to the injured area. It also has the disadvantage of breaking the skin and allowing infection. Other forms of violent therapy are open to the same objection. Vasodilator agents[7] do not improve tissue survival, nor are the results of sympathectomy striking.[8, 9] The use of dextran sufficiently early to prevent sludging will rarely be practicable, and there is some possibility of danger in its use.[10, 11] Possibly at sea level the use of hyperbaric oxygen or at altitude that of supplementary oxygen[12, 13] may increase tissue tension of oxygen and just tip the balance in the favour of a cell partially damaged by cold injury.

Warming seems to be the most effective treatment, with rapid warming showing less loss of tissue than slow warming,[14, 15, 16] possibly because the area of circulatory arrest is smaller after rapid warming,[17] damage to the blood vessels is less, and there is less sludging.[18] Warming has the additional advantage that it can relatively easily be done on the spot—so shortening the time that the blood vessels and cells remain frozen and exposed to temperatures at which high electrolyte concentrations are dangerous. Once active rewarming has been started it seems doubtful whether any other active treatment is of benefit.

All cases diagnosed as frostbite should be treated either at a well-equipped camp, from which evacuation by air or some other means is easy, or in a hospital. Attempts to treat frostbite at high camps or anywhere with inadequate facilities are ill-advised. No attempt should be made to treat the frostbitten part except under ideal conditions, as once rewarming has started the tissues are liable to infection and may die. No patient should be allowed to walk on thawed or partly thawed feet. Walking on frostbitten feet does not appear to increase the liability to tissue loss, and may be the best method of reaching safety.

Code of Practice

Treatment should be directed at both the whole individual and the affected part. The most important factor in treating the whole individual is to keep morale high. Generalized rewarming may be necessary, as some hypothermia is almost inevitable, especially at high altitude. This is best carried out by giving hot liquids or even oxygen. The patient must be put in a sleeping bag and an extra source of heat may be provided by his companions lying alongside him in a sleeping bag, or in the same sleeping bag. If hypothermia and frostbite co-exist, the treatment of hypothermia should have priority.

Food should be given, as in itself it causes some peripheral vasodilation. Alcohol may also be given, but only if some time is to be spent in shelter. It will cause vasodilation — but more important will boost morale and diminish any pain caused by the rewarming. A broad-spectrum antibiotic should be started as a prophylactic against infection, while mild analgesics such as aspirin may be used to alleviate pain.

The affected part should be warmed, preferably using a container with water at 44°C. To measure the temperature accurately a thermometer should be available, as water that is too hot will damage the limb. If a thermometer is not available the temperature should be tested with a normal, unfrostbitten finger. If too hot for comfort more cold water should be added. The temperature of the water should never be tested with a frostbitten finger, because this will be partially anaesthetic owing to nerve injury. If no container is available, hot water poured over towels, or a cloth wrapped around the part may be used.

Rewarming should last about 20 minutes at a time; the temperature of the water should be checked frequently to see that it does not fall below 42°C. Additional hot water should not be poured over the affected part.

If rewarming by fluid is impossible, the part should be placed against a warm abdomen, armpit, or held in warm air. It should never be placed by an open fire as, again, it is partially anaesthetized and can be burnt without pain.

After rewarming, the part should be cleaned. But, because the tissues are extremely friable and liable to infection if broken, dirt must be removed gradually and gently. Blisters should be left, and should not be pricked or

24

removed as they form a covering. Nevertheless, some blisters may be broken, and soft dry absorbent dressing should be used as cover. Similar dressings between the fingers or toes will prevent friction and prevent further damage to the skin. Even light pressure can cause pressure sores, infection, and loss of tissue.

So long as the affected part is warm and does not get rubbed it may be kept exposed. Swelling may occur, and this can be countered by raising the part. Local antibiotics may be used but it is unwise to rely on this method alone for combating infection. No tissue should be removed surgically for three main reasons: it is impossible to assess the depth of frostbitten tissue; the black carapace acts as a protective covering for regenerating tissue; and premature surgery appears to have been the most potent cause of the poor results of treatment. Active movements should be carried out to prevent joint stiffening, and if these are not possible, passive movement should be employed.

Progress

Surgical intervention must be minimal. The blackened carapace will gradually separate by itself without interference. Efforts to hasten separation are usually ill-advised and are   more likely to lead to infection, loss of tissue, and delay in healing rather than the reverse.

Too few cases are seen by any individual and there is a tendency to try more than one treatment in the hope that more rapid healing will occur. In general, however, provided there is no surgical intervention, most cases of frostbite seem to heal in six to twelve months.

Prognosis

The prognosis should be guarded, but optimistic, as the gangrenous tissue is essentially superficial. Thus in one patient with bilateral gangrene of the feet extending to the ankles, conservative treatment resulted in a complete recovery without tissue loss in nine months. In another patient, both of whose legs were essentially blocks of frozen tissue to above the knees when first seen, conservative treatment for about a year resulted in recovery except for patches of persistent gangrene on the heels. Bilateral amputation was carried out for this reason alone.

Probably many unnecessary amputations have been carried out because of impatience at the very slow recovery. The gangrenous carapace may persist for months, and the failure to appreciate that it is a 'superficial' rather than a 'deep' gangrene may lead to precipitate surgery.

Once a part is frostbitten, it is more liable to cold injury on subsequent occasions. The skin may crack when dry, even at normal temperature, causing painful fissures in the pulps of the thumb and fingers. The use of a hand cream at regular intervals will soften the skin.

References

1 Ward, M.P. *British Medical Journal,* 1974. *1,* 67.
2 Washburn, B., *New England Journal of Medicine,* 1962. *266,* 974.
3 Pugh, L.G. in *The Physiology of Human Survival,* ed. O. G. Edholm and
   A. L. Bacharach, New York and London. Academic Press, 1965.
4 Greene, R. *Journal of Pathology and Bacteriology,* 1943, *55,* 259.
5 Durand, J., and Martineaud, J.P., in *High Altitude Physiology,* ed.
   R. Porter and Knight. Churchill Livingstone, 1971.
6 Hartley, L.H., Alexander, J.K., Modelski, M., and Grover, R.F.,
   Journal of Applied Physiology, 1967, *23,* 839.
7 Shumaker, H.B., Radigan, L.R., Haskell, H., Ziperman, H.H., and Hughes, R.R.,
   Angiology, 1951, *2,* 100.
8 Golding, M.R., Mendoza, M.F., Hennigar, G.R., Fries, C.C., and Wesolowski,
   S.A., *Surgery,* 1964, *56,* 221.
9 Gildenberg, P.L., and Hardenbergh, E., *Annals of Surgery,* 1964, *160,* 160.
10 Mundth, E.D., Long, D.M., and Brown, R.B., *Journal of Trauma,* 1964, *4,*
   246.
11 Anderson, R.A., and Hardenbergh, E., *Journal of Surgical Research,* 1965, *5,*
   256.
12 Greene, R., *Lancet,* 1941, *2,* 689.
13 Ward, M.P., Garnham, J.R., Simpson, B.R.J., and Morley, G.H., and Winter,
   J.N., *Proceedings of Royal Society of Medicine,* 1968, *61,* 787.
14 Harkins, H.N., and Harmon, P.H., *Journal of Clinical Investigation,* 1937, *16,*
   213.
15 Finneran, J.C., and Shumacker, H.B., *Surgery, Gynecology and Obstetrics
   with International Abstracts of Surgery,* 1950, *90,* 430.
16 Fuhrman, F.A., and Fuhrman, G.J., *Medicine,* 1957, *36,* 465.
17 Crismon, J.M., and Fuhrman, F.A., *Journal of Clinical Investigation,* 1947, *26,*
   468.
18 Aturson, G., *Acta Chirurigica Scandinavica,* 1966, *131,* 402.

Discussion

Dr. Houston raised the dilemma posed by a hypothermic patient with frostbite.
Should the hypothermia be treated immediately and the frostbite left, or vice
versa?

Dr. Ward expressed an inclination to treat the hypothermia and leave the
frostbite. The rationale of this was the overwhelming advantage of retaining
mobility in the patient. It was time-consuming, difficult and dangerous to move
patients on high mountains other than by their own efforts. Hypothermia is
lethal; frostbite is not.

Dr. F. Jackson emphasised the need to prevent mechanical injury to frostbitten limbs.

Dr. Nelms. Two weeks ago I saw two very serious frostbite cases in Canada.
Thermography apparatus of ours showed living tissue well distal to the line of
surface demarcation. Removal of tissue would have been quite wrong.

Prof. Odell. 50 years ago in 1924 on Everest Dr. T.H. Somervell was altogether against amputation. In his view it was far better to try to save the limb.

Dr. F. Jackson observed that surgery made the effects of frostbite worse (if done immediately).

Prof. Williams referred to the subjective sensations of mild cold injury. He thought that before the onset of cold injury a limb might be painful for a long time. What steps do you then take at this stage?

Dr. Clarke, speaking from recent experience had had no premonitary pain and observed that it was imperative to rest the affected part and that it was essential to impress upon the patient how serious frostbite was and how necessary it was to prevent traumatic injury.

Avoidance of Cold Injury:
An Outline of Basic Principles

JOHN JACKSON

The following environmental factors need to be taken into account, the appropriate protection being indicated:—

1.	Cold/Lapse Rate	— (a)	Layers of insulating air and materials.
2.	Wind	— (b)	Wind proofs
3.	Rain	— (c)	Water proofs
4.	Water Vapour	— (d)	Materials permeable to water vapour.

1. *Pure cold* and/or the effects of the lapse rate *i.e.* a temperature drop that can vary between 3°F and 7°F. per 1,000 ft. dependent on conditions.

Action

(a)   Wear garments that enable a layer, or better still, several layers of warm air to circulate between the skin and the cold air outside. Many modern sophisticated garments using principles of airflow, basically do the same job as wearing three layers of Shetland Wool sweaters. Another example is the use of straw and dried mosses by Lapps and Tibetans inside their boots. The same basic principle is incorporated in the modern High Altitude boots.

2. *Effects of wind* plus cold are drastic. e.g. A temperature of $+ 20^{O}$F and a wind of 45 m.p.h. is equivalent to a temperature of $- 40^{O}$F and a breeze of 2 m.p.h.

Action

(b)   It is essential that the external wind is unable to enter the garments and

28

thereby replace the warm air microclimate surrounding the person. The cold moving air would cause a dramatic loss of heat. Therefore mountaineers, skiers etc., require clothing materials that are windproof. Examples of such materials have been the Nylon/Cotton anoraks as used on high mountains such as Everest and Kanchenjunga. Some centres in Britain used Nylon/Cotton in the 50's and early 60's but for important reasons replaced these with more durable and waterproof materials. Ventile type materials are windproof, permeable to water vapour, and are to a degree waterproof. The native materials i.e. Tibetan Chuba, Kashmir tweed etc., work in similar fashion.

3. *In a cold/wet climate* it is clear that unless waterproof garments are used the cold rain will quickly replace the warm, circulating, insulating air. Water conducts heat away from the body very quickly.

Action

(c) Use waterproof as well as windproof materials. Essential in the British mountains which have a very hostile cold/wet climate. E.g. In the Scawfell Cirque of the Lake District or the Snowdon Basin of North Wales the average annual rainfall is around 250 inches i.e. they are the wettest basins in Europe. As most of the rain falls at the same time as a prevailing S.W. wind it can be seen that Chill Index factor plays a formidable part in cooling.

4. *If materials do not breathe* i.e. are not permeable to water vapour the body sweat or condensation will take the place of the warm insulating air.

Action

(d) Clothing materials should be permeable to water vapour. In cold/dry climates this requirement is more readily complied with. In cold/wet climates the need for waterproof as well as windproof materials poses a problem and in the main a compromise has to be made. In the sphere of training and experience provision people need to be shown and encouraged to use clothing sensibly i.e. clothing can be taken off as required and replaced when necessary. This taking off and putting on of garments is essential with the modern cheaper materials that do not breathe.

Other important points

Garments should not be tight thereby restricting blood flow.

Materials that do not compress readily are much to be preferred, e.g. sleeping bag materials; use of mesh insoles inside boots.

Feet and Hands are particularly susceptible to cold injury.

Feet. Use good boots with insulation properties, good wool socks, mesh insoles, overboots or gaiters.

Hands. Thin silk gloves, wool for over gloves and good windproof over mitts are essential.

Adherence to good routine of food/fuel intake is essential.

However good the equipment its correct use is essential.

Personal physical tone/fitness is important.

Mental fitness is a most important factor.

How to Avoid Cold Injury

D. G. ROBERTSON and JOHN JACKSON

This contribution to the Symposium took the form of a demonstration of techniques and protective clothing. A comprehensive exhibition of relevant equipment was on view.

Discussion

Brig. Marchant. 'Ventile' has been in production since 1943. It is the only material in the world which will meet the British Standard Specification on waterproofness. 50 inches of pressure has been reached by Ventile. That is, if a tube has the end covered with this cloth it can be filled with water to a height of 50 inches before the fabric begins to allow water to pass through it.

A contributor to the discussion stated that in the mid 1960's a firm produced a fabric called RIVA which they claimed would be vapour permeable and yet would not let much water in. It was not developed.

Medical and Physiological Investigations on Mountaineers

A field study during a winter climb in the Bernese Oberland.

E. LEUTHOLD, G. HARTMANN, R. BÜHLMANN, H. MATTHYS, H. OBERLI, U. WIGET, P. ASTRUP

Mountaineering in the Alps has become a mass sport. The physiological and medical problems related to it are therefore of great interest. Most of the research work done in mountain medicine in recent decades has however been focused on problems of very high altitudes such as found in the Himalayas or in the Andes. Relatively little attention has been paid to conditions of medium altitudes, to nutrition, fluid balance, limits to performance and finally to behaviour under extreme conditions of stress and cold.

It was for this reason that in 1969 the Swiss Foundation for Alpine Research sponsored an interdisciplinary study during a winter climb under expedition conditions in the Bernese Oberland, Switzerland.

The whole project was conceived as a pilot study in order to clarify the feasibility of such a study as well as to find out which problems deserved most scientific attention.

Method

The project was carried out on six top climbers who volunteered as subjects, spending 14 days of very difficult climbing in altitudes between 3500 and 4000 metres, carrying an average load of 25 kg and being exposed to an average temperature of -13° Centigrade. The party was accompanied by a photographer who made a very informative film. The tests done before and after the climb were carried out at the Department of Medicine of the University of Basel. During the climb the laboratory facilities of the Altitude Research Station at Jungfraujoch were used.

The main objects of the study were:
- balance of energy (calories), nitrogen, water and electrolytes.
- effects of two different types of food, one rich in carbohydrates, the other rich in proteins and fat.
- spiroergometry to test the capacity of physical performance.

- acclimatization as defined by the 2,3 -diphosphoglycerates (DPG).
- psychological tests in order to test the psychosocial and psychomotor behaviour.

Furthermore practically all the important laboratory parameters as well as clinical data were collected in order to get as complete a medical picture as possible and to find out possible trends. Thus the laboratory examinations comprised complete haematology, coagulation factors, glucose tolerance tests, ECG and even gastric secretion studies. A medical history, a complete physical examination and continued medical surveillance were included.

The subjects were given exactly calculated food rations. They had to keep a record of their consumption of food and fluid and they had to collect all their urine in daily portions. Contact was maintained by radio, helicopter and direct approach by the medical team.

Results

Clinical data

Amazingly enough none of the volunteers was found to be in 'perfect health' to begin with. In spite of their proven top performance in mountaineering a host of more or less important findings was detected, such as psoriasis, severe spondylosis, arthrosis, a diabetic glucose tolerance test and a juvenile hyperbilirubinemia. During the climb upper respiratory tract infections and mild frost bite occurred. One climber collapsed and had to be evacuated by helicopter from an altitude of 4,000 metres. Exposure and exhaustion was found to be the cause.

Nutrition, calorie and nitrogen balance

The most surprising and unexpected finding was strikingly deficient nutrition. In the best case the intake covered 65%, in the worst only 35% of the calculated calorie requirements. The two different diets yielded neither objective nor subjective advantages. All climbers would have preferred a mixed diet. None of them was able to maintain a positive nitrogen balance. Body weight and measurements of skin folds showed that the calorie deficit was covered exclusively from fat stores. The degree of inadequacy of food intake correlated with an insufficient fluid intake and with the degree of exhaustion.

Water and electrolyte metabolism

The fluid intake was also totally inadequate and ranged from 1,400 ml to 2,100 ml per day as a mean. The reason was, that all the water had to be gained by melting snow with solid or liquid fuel which had to be carried. The daily output of urine was correspondingly low and lay between 400 and 800 ml. Sodium and potassium balance were negative with one exception. There was considerable microcrystaluria during the days with low fluid intake but no proteinuria. The hematocrit showed that fluid loss occured in the extravascular compartment.

Further laboratory data

Among a host of interesting results worth being discussed, the following may be mentioned: a considerable rise of Lactic Dehydrogenase and Creatine Phosphokinase believed to be due to muscular activity and microtrauma, a general drop of the serum lipids and an increased glucose tolerance at the end of the test, probably secondary to the weight loss.

The basal gastric secretion revealed no significant changes whereas the fasting amounts were clearly elevated at altitude. A decreased rate of gastric emptying might be the reason for it.

Respiration and circulation

Comparative ergospirometric measurements before, during and after the test failed to reveal any increase of the physical working capacity (average 250—280 Watt). The partial oxygen pressure in the arterialised capillary blood and the static pulmonary volumes, however, were improved. It could be clearly demonstrated that up to altitudes of 4,000 metres it was the cardiac adaptation which became the limiting factor to a further increase of physical performance and not the ventilatory capacity of the lungs. There was also a good correlation between the individual capacity of physical performance as measured by bicycle ergometry in the laboratory and the later performance on the mountains.

Psychological studies

After a thorough psychological history the climbers were submitted to extensive testing of their intelligence structure, concentration, manual skill and social behaviour. The results revealed extremely different characteristics, ranging from labile and irritable to steadfast and stable. During the tough climb it was obvious that two of the lesser intelligent ones worked their way up in the group thanks to their practical skill and steadiness. One member of the party could never fully integrate whereas two moved from the periphery of mutual esteem to its centre. A very democratic style of leadership was maintained throughout the two weeks. The forecast of psychological behaviour on the basis of the initial tests proved amazingly accurate.

Conclusions

One of the most striking aspects of this study was the rapidity with which objective symptoms of physical deterioration set in. The inadequate fluid intake may have been one of the first and most important reasons for this. A daily fluid intake of three to four litres, therefore, is of paramount importance or else an insufficient caloric intake will be the consequence with ensuing metabolic disturbances. The climber must spend the necessary time and effort on providing fluid, even if it should be at the expense of climbing time and sleep.

The controversy on the advantages of a carbohydrate rich or a protein rich diet is obsolete. A mixed and palatable diet is most likely to guarantee the maintenance of a positive metabolic balance.

The adaptation to medium altitudes, up to 4000 metres, is rapid and does not require any special training in young and healthy subjects. Maximum performances, however, should not be attempted before an acclimatisation period of 24 to 48 hours.

The capacity of physical performance can be estimated with fair accuracy by ergospirometric tests. This should be done when preparing for an expedition.

A good group performance, as required during a long climb or an expedition, depends largely on the personality structure and the psychosocial behaviour of the climbers. The tests used in this study proved useful and should also be used when selecting members for an expedition.

Finally it was obvious that a "clean bill of health" is not an absolute requirement for top performance in the mountains. The importance of motivation and mental endurance is amazing and just as important as physical fitness.

The whole project proved not only the feasability of such a field study but also its necessity. Many of the results conflict with reported work from laboratory studies in exercise physiology or with known traditions and beliefs. The extreme climber in the Alps is exposed to various adverse factors, such as physical and psychological stress, cold and fatigue. The mild hypoxia of medium altitudes and its effects are usually negligible. The problems of exposure to cold dominate. More research work is needed to further clarify many of the questions raised. It is hoped that it will soon be done to the benefit of Alpinism and for all those who practice it.

*This study has been published in German in the form of a monograph:
Hartmann G., Alpiner Hochleistungstest, Verlag Hans Huber, Bern, 1973.

This contribution to the symposium took the form of a silent colour film with commentary by Dr. Leuthold. It illustrated the conditions of the expedition lasting a few days from its start at the Eiger station on the Jungfraujoch mountain railway to its end in the Lötschental. Dr. Leuthold explained that the scientific results had been published in a series of papers each dealing with a particular aspect of the study.

Discussion

Professor Williams drew attention to the significance of the fact that it was the leader who collapsed. His own work suggested that a leader was not a good physiological subject because of the extra stress imposed upon him.

Dr. Leuthold. Yes, but in this case the leadership was largely democratic.

Dr. Rennie. Did not everything (viz. all the trouble) flow from a lack of food on your expedition?

Dr. Leuthold. Not the improved glucose tolerance. Why should that occur because of dietary restraint? What did Professor Williams' people do on their scientific expedition by way of exercise?

Professor Williams. Only enough to stop boredom. We wanted to study hypoxia. We wanted to exclude exercise as a problem.

Dr. Leuthold. We wanted to keep hypoxia out of it.

Mr. Ward. The symptoms you described were very like those we had on Everest. There, of course, you definitely had hypoxia added to them.

Professor Williams wished that those who gave financial grants for this type of field work had seen the extraordinary effort that it took to get results. Then they would recognise how amazing it was to get results at all.

Dr. Lloyd. In 1974 we measured in runners both weight loss and proteinuria and we found that hose who had the greatest weight loss also had the most protein in their urine.

Dr. Rennie. I found that you can calculate how high someone is by measuring the quantity of protein in his urine.

Professor Hervey. Continuous exposure to *cold* (which may be quite mild) leads to dehydration, which is of the body fluid volume depletion type shown by very high haematocrit values. This occurs even though fluid intake is adequate. In this case there is a diuresis over the first day or two of exposure. Hence, to prevent dehydration — which must impair performance and which also predisposes to cold injury — it is necessary to have equipment capable of completely protecting from cold as well as encouraging drinking.

Dr. Nelms. Were you (Dr. Leuthold) able to follow up your study of food replacement? *We* did it for a period of up to 14 days. It was astonishing to see how the subjects replaced food in less than 48 hours: 7,000 calories per day.

Dr. Leuthold. We only checked three days. Subjects had not recovered weight loss.

Professor Moore. Is fluid loss more quickly replaced than calorie loss?

Dr. Leuthold. Yes, but there was an inadvertent replacement half way through the expedition at the Jungfraujoch.

Mountaineering and the Endocrine System

E. S. WILLIAMS

In terms of evolution the endocrine system is very old; even the most primitive animals have a regulating system based upon the secretion of particular substances which diffuse to, or are carried by a circulatory system to parts of the organism where they have a specific action. In the higher animals, including man, specialized cells are gathered into identifiable entities called glands each secreting one or more of such substances, called hormones, directly into the blood stream. The blood thus contains many such hormones, most being present in minute quantities and each having highly specific actions. In many cases a particular hormone acts only at a specialized site in the body and has no influence elsewhere; hormones are thus 'chemical messengers' in this complex regulatory system.

Of the two principal systems of control of bodily functions — the nervous system, and the endocrine system — the nervous system is by far the most important as regards survival in the extreme conditions encountered on mountains. Whether it is a matter of surviving cold exposure, extreme fatigue, or hypoxia, or of ensuring appropriate food and fluid intake it is the use of the brain which, in man, tips the balance between his ability to survive and his succumbing to the adverse environment. This use of the brain and the nervous system implies forethought as regards artificial protection of an essentially fragile body and training, so that not only is the neuro-muscular system in the best condition to respond to extreme demands upon it, but also the optimum psychological approach is achieved to the dangers and challenge of the environment. Fear in the form of long-term apprehension should be eliminated although fear in an emergency situation, suitably controlled by the conscious will, has an important survival value.

The endocrine system is closely linked with the brain and the functional state of some endocrine glands is markedly influenced by the emotions. Hence the 'attitude of mind' of the person exposed to an adverse environment can affect the endocrine response to that environment. Although the endocrine system plays an essential part in aiding bodily adjustments to adverse conditions, in man it plays a supplementary role in the context of the survival of the fit mountaineer. What follows should be read with this in mind.

Low environment temperature

The importance of the heat produced by the body, 'animal heat', has been recognized from time immemorial but only during this century has its source been recognized in detail. Certain structures within the cells of the body are the site of the controlled oxidation of foodstuffs, the chemical reactions concerned producing not only the chemical compounds required by the body, but also heat. Thyroid hormone regulates the steady state oxygen consumption and hence this heat-production mechanism. Heat arises as a result of other processes but for practical purposes one can consider that virtually 'all the heat generated in the resting animal is a result of this oxidation process and the effect is referred to as "thyroid thermogenesis". (1)

Much recent work on animals has shown that the immediate response of the body to a lowered temperature is mediated by an increased activity of the adrenal glands. In many that part of these glands known as the medulla appears to respond rapidly and the outer part, the cortex, which has a separate function, responds shortly afterwards. (2) In man exposed to cold the body temperature rises, as does the blood pressure and the pulse rate and all the 'defences' against body cooling are probably a result of the immediate adrenal medullary response to the cold stress. If the body begins to cool then the adrenal appears to respond poorly. (3) For this reason the emergency administration of adrenal hormones to mountaineers in a state of collapse as a result of exposure has been advocated. (4)

Until recently it was therefore considered that the thyroid controlled the 'background' or resting heat production and if it responded to a cold stress it did so only over a very long term. An experiment carried out on four men in the Antarctic showed that the concentration in the blood of one of the thyroid hormones, triiodothyronine (T_3), rose significantly by the second day of cold exposure and of the other thyroid hormone, thyroxine, by the third to the fourth day. (5) Recent work suggests that the important index of thyroid activity is the concentration in the blood of that part of the total T_3 which is unbound to proteins, the 'free' fraction. A single experiment carried out by the author showed that within one hour of taking 120 microgrammes of T_3 by mouth the concentration of both protein-bound and free T_3 in his blood had risen by a factor of almost four times the initial value (fig. 1). Further work is in progress on this finding but it suggests that heat production could be usefully stimulated by administration of T_3.

Hypoxia

When insufficient oxygen is available to the body a series of changes are at once apparent and provided the degree of oxygen lack, or hypoxia as it is called, is not too severe the body adjusts to the changed conditions and the healthy person is capable of normal activity. When this has occurred the person is said to be acclimatized. It is only in about the last two decades that significant work has been done on the effects of hypoxia on the endocrine system of the body and on the contribution of this system to the adjustments which result in acclimatization.

The principal known direct effects of oxygen lack on the endocrine system are on the adrenal cortex and on the endocrine function of the kidneys. It is probable that the rise in the secretion of the adrenal cortical hormone, cortisol, which has been demonstrated, is a non-specific response to the "stress" on the body of the hypoxia but that the marked changes in the handling of the essential elements sodium and potassium which are under the control of another adrenal cortical hormone, aldosterone, is a specific effect. This was first demonstrated by indirect methods in 1956 (6), more directly confirmed in 1960 (7,8) and in 1966 (9,10) by directly measuring under hypoxic conditions the secretion rate of these two hormones by the adrenal cortex. While the secretion rate of cortisol increases, that of aldosterone markedly decreases. As acclimatization proceeds these changes revert to normal.

Later work showed that the kidney hormone known as renin had greater activity in the blood on sudden exposure to hypoxia and that this effect positively correlated with heart rate changes. It is possible that the primary change is within the cardiovascular system, this giving rise to the renin changes and not vice versa (11).

Mountaineers have long known that at high altitude they have a marked preference for sweet foods. It is therefore of interest to observe that during one of the author's field studies at the moderate altitude of 3500 metres the concentration of glucose in the blood in five men increased at this altitude (fig. 2). It is interesting to observe that at the same time the average blood insulin concentration in these men also rose (see table). The diet was strictly controlled during the whole period of the study, both before, during, and after the ascent; the degree of physical activity was also uniform during the three periods; and the blood samples were all taken after overnight fasting at the same time each day.

Although many investigators have carried out studies of the endocrine system in relation to an adverse environment much of this work has been done on animals. More work is now being done on men and mountaineers can expect further useful knowledge to accrue during the next few years.

Practical Suggestions

These relate to fit healthy people exposed to an adverse environment and *not* to elderly, frail, hypothermic patients.

1. In view of the close inter-relation of the brain with the endocrine system the person likely to be exposed to extreme conditions should be well trained so that fear is eliminated.

2. Triiodothyronine could be carried for *emergency use* only when accidental hypothermia is probable. Optimum dosage is subject to further study.

-3. Both triiodothyronine and an adrenal steriod should be given immediately intravenously by the medical man first on the scene where a hypothermic casualty is being rescued.

4. A diet for high altitude climbing should be high in carbohydrates; sugar as such and in the form of sweets, etc., should be provided in adequate quantity.

5. High altitude oedema in its various forms is likely to be closely linked to the endocrine response to hypoxia. Prevention and treatment of this serious complication of exposure to hypoxia is well understood and is dealt with elsewhere in this symposium.

References

1 EDELMAN, I.S., Thyroid Thermogenesis. *New Eng. J. Med.* 1974, *290*, 1303–1308.
2 SUZUKI, M., TONOUE, T., MATSUZAKI, S., YAMAMOTO, K., Initial Response of Human Thyroid, Adrenal Cortex, and Adrenal Medulla to Acute Cold Exposure. *Can. J. Physiol. Pharmacol.*, 1967, *45*, 423–432.
3 WOOLF, P.D., HOLLANDER, C.S., Endocrine Response to Accidental Cold Exposure in Man. *Clin. Res.* 1971, *19*, 385.
4 MACINNES, C.M., ROTHWELL, R.I., JACOBS, H.S., NABARRO, J.D.N., Plasma-11-Hydroxycorticosteroid and Growth Hormone levels in Climbers. *Lancet* 1971, *1*, 49–51.
5 EASTMAN, C.J., EKINS, R.P., LEITH, I.M., WILLIAMS, E.S., Thyroid Hormone Response to Prolonged Cold Exposure in Man. *J. Physiol.* 1974, *241*, 175–181.
6 WILLIAMS, E.S., Salivary Electrolyte Composition at High Altitude; *Clin. Sci.*, 1961, *21*, 37–42.
7 AYRES, P.J., HURTER, R.C., WILLIAMS, E.S., RUNDO, J. Aldosterone Excretion and Potassium Retention in Subjects Living at High Altitude; *Nature,* 1961, *191*, 78.
8 WILLIAMS, E.S. Electrolyte Regulation during the Adaptation of Humans to Life at High Altitude; *Proc. Roy. Soc.* B., 1966, *165,* 266–280.
9 SLATER, J.D.H., WILLIAMS, E.S., EDWARDS, R.H.T., EKINS, R.P., SÖNKSEN, P.H., BERESFORD, C.H., McLAUGHLIN, M. Potassium Retention during the Respiratory Alkalosis of Mild Hypoxia in Man: its relationship to Aldosterone Secretion and other Metabolic Changes; *Clin. Sci.* 1969, *37*, 311–326.

10 SLATER, J.D.H., TUFFLEY, R.E., WILLIAMS, E.S., BERESFORD, C.H., SÖNKSEN, P.H., EDWARDS, R.H.T., EKINS, R.P., McLAUCHLIN, M. Control of Aldosterone Secretion during Acclimatization in Hypoxia in Man; *Clin. Sci.* 1969, *37*, 327–341.

11 TUFFLEY, R.E., RUBENSTEIN, D., SLATER, J.D.H., WILLIAMS, E.S., Serum Renin Activity during Exposure to Hypoxia; *J. Endocrin.* 1970, *48*, 497–510.

Insulin concentration in microunits per millilitre of blood serum in 5 men studied before, during, and after an air-lift ascent to 3500 metres altitude.

MOUNTAINEER	A	B	C	D	E
Before Ascent					
Days blood samples obtained	4	4	4	4	4
Mean insulin concentration	9.00	19.00	19.71	12.88	6.62
	±	±	±	±	±
Standard deviation	3.00	2.87	2.92	3.95	1.84
At 3500 m					
Days blood samples obtained	4	4	4	4	4
Mean insulin concentration	11.71	21.25	21.00	12.75	10.50
	±	±	±	±	±
Standard deviation	4.30	5.23	3.88	4.65	4.30
After Descent					
Days blood samples obtained	4	5	5	5	5
Mean insulin concentration	8.75	14.40	21.50	12.22	7.20
	±	±	±	±	±
Standard deviation	1.38	3.89	5.58	5.21	2.48

A paired t test on the null hypothesis that ascent gave rise to no change gave: $t = 2.9$; $v = 4$; $p = 0.044$.

Details of the periods at various altitudes, dietary control, and related data are included in reference (9) but the results in this table have not previously been published. They are derived from assay data provided by Dr. P. H. Sönksen, a member of the field party.

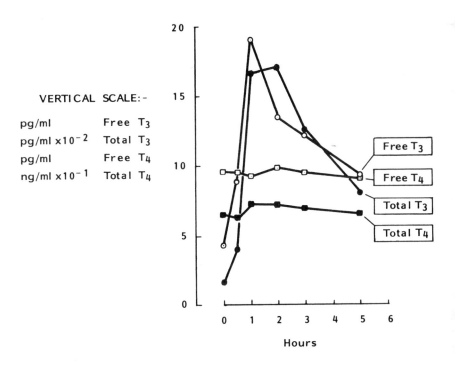

VERTICAL SCALE:-

pg/ml	Free T₃
pg/ml ×10⁻²	Total T₃
pg/ml	Free T₄
ng/ml ×10⁻¹	Total T₄

Figure 1

A preliminary experiment on one man showing the concentration in his blood of the two thyroid hormones, triiodothyronine (T_3) and thyroxine (T_4) following his taking an oral dose of T_3. (Note: one pg = one picogramme = 1×10^{-12} gramme; one ng = one nanogramme = 1×10^{-9} gramme).

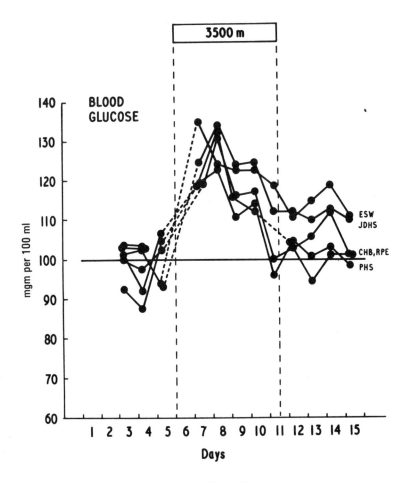

Figure 2

Graphs showing the concentration in the blood of glucose in five men before, during, and after an effortless ascent to 3500 metres altitude. Each blood sample was taken at the same time of day after overnight fasting.

Adrenocortical Activity in High Altitude Climbing

J. WOLF

Sport performance of any kind can be considered to be a sign of adaptation of the organism as a whole and of the sum of individual organ systems. In performances connected with great objective risk the diencephalo-hypophyso-adrenal system is highly engaged and is responsible for optimal response to load. It appears especially in such sport disciplines in which heavy load is caused by extreme external conditions, by the risk factor of the performance itself or finally by the time of the subject's exposure to the mentioned conditions.

We followed the function of the diencephalo-hypophyso-adrenal system by means of some indirect tests in sportsmen exposed during performance to environmental factors, to time factor as well as to the factor of high risk. In some cases we tried to correlate the results obtained with the results of the same tests in sports influenced less by these factors and eventually with results of simple functional tests of the circulatory system.

As indicators of the function of the diencephalo-hypophyso-adrenal system we used:

1. Absolute numbers of eosinophils in peripheral blood according to Thorn before and after load.

2. Changes of fragility of skin capillaries by the sucking method of Verbely before and after load.

3. Level of catecholamine metabolites excreted in urine before, during and after load lasting for a long time and combined with high risk factor.

Results

1. Eosinophil counts were made before and after load in three groups:
   a) women rowers; mainly physical load − training.
   b) parachutists; mainly risk load − descent by parachute from the plane.
   c) mountain climbers; combined load − technically difficult climbing, lasting a long time in winter conditions.

45

According to Thorn a decrease of 75% is significant as representing changes in the organism. The mountain climbers showed an average only slightly above this limit. Some individuals had greater losses and it was concluded that this load will cause in more than one third of cases a critical loss of eosinophils.

2. The fragility of capillaries decreases or remains practically unchanged after a mainly technical load such as gymnastics. Load due to a long exposure to stress causes considerable increase of the number of petechiae per square centimetre.

3. In the first phase of climbing the curves of urinary vanillylmandelic (VMA) and homovanillic (HVA) acids follow the curve of the circulation test. During the time of maximal stress — reaching an altitude of 7,135 m the HVA curve continues to decline while the VMA curve increases. This is explained by the changes leading from tyrosine via dihydroxyphenylalanine and dopamine to homovanillic acid on the one hand, and on the other hand via noradrenaline and adrenaline to vanillylmandelic acid. The metabolic pathways causing a higher production of noradrenaline and adrenaline, as indicated by the level of vanillylmandelic acid in urine, prevailed over the metabolic pathway from dopamine or even directly from dihydroxyphenylalanine to homovanillic acid. The metabolic process shifted toward the synthesis of noradrenaline and adrenaline probably to enable the circulation to make up for the lower partial pressure of oxygen, and physical and psychological stress.

Recommendations

Our observations enable us to come to preventive and therapeutic conclusions. It also shows that simple functional tests of the circulatory system can give a wrong idea about the real situation of the organism as a whole. In every sport performance — especially in high altitude climbing — there are circumstances which can load the mechanism of adaptability to such an extent that the stress becomes supramaximal and the performance can end fatally. In such accidents it is necessary to apply substitutional administration of adrenal gland hormones.

Note
This paper is a summary of work carried out by Dr. Wolf and his colleagues from Prague.

Nutrition: A general review for the Mountaineer

GASTON L. S. PAWAN

For the maintenance of health, normal body weight, and nutritional status, the daily diet should contain a sufficiency of the nutrients in correct amounts and relative proportions. The nutrients, i.e., proteins, fats, carbohydrates, minerals and vitamins, are normally obtained by the consumption of wholesome foodstuffs in the form of nutritionally-balanced, palatable, and readily-digested meals. Tables of Recommended Intakes of Nutrients for the U.K. have been published by the Department of Health and Social Security (1969). Similar tables have been published by several other countries. The average moderately-active healthy man in the U.K. of normal (70kg) body composition (Table 1) obtains some 3000 Kcal. from food, daily. (1 Kcal = 4.184 kJ.). His calories are made up of 50–60% carbohydrates, 30–40% Fat, and 10–15% protein. An approximation of his principal daily nutrient requirements and their main functions are as follows:

Protein

Proteins are the fundamental structural components of all cells. Everyone must have a good supply to build, repair, and maintain body tissues; to form hormones which regulate body metabolism; to manufacture antibodies which combat infection and to synthesize enzymes which control the rate of biochemical processes in the body. A large proportion of the protein in the body is found in the 25 kg. or so, of muscle tissue (about 40% body weight). Proteins are combinations of some twenty-two amino acids. Most of these can be manufactured by the body from other foods. However, there are eight amino acids which cannot be made by the body, and must be supplied by dietary protein. Food protein containing all the essential amino acids are called complete proteins, and are of 'high biological value'. Animal proteins, like meat, poultry, eggs, fish, milk and cheese, are complete proteins. Vegetable products, like cereals, nuts, bread, beans and peas are good sources of protein, but like all vegetables are deficient in one, or more, of the essential amino acids, i.e., are incomplete protein foods.

47

The pure vegetarian (vegan) must, therefore, eat a variety of different vegetable protein foods to ensure he obtains his full quota of all the essential amino acids. Recently, a variety of texturised vegetable protein has been made available. These substances contain all the essential amino acids. Protein, if burned in the body provides 4 Kcal. per gram ($\equiv 17kJ/gram$).

Fats

These are the most concentrated source of energy, yielding some 9 Kcal. per gram ($\equiv 37kJ/gram$). Fatty foods are necessary for providing palatability and satiety and furnish the fat soluble vitamins, A, D, E, K, and the essential fatty acids, mainly linoleic acid. The fatty acids found in fats and oils are either saturated or unsaturated. In general, animal fats are high in saturated fatty acids while vegetable oils are high in poly-unsaturated fatty acids. There are exceptions to this rule, as poultry and fish fat is fairly unsaturated, while the vegetable oils in the coconut and palm are mostly saturated. In recent years, much attention has been focused on the possible role of an excessive intake of saturated (animal) fats in the aetiology of atheroma and coronary heart disease. There is some statistical epidemiological evidence that the incidence of coronary attacks and blood cholesterol levels in men, are higher in populations consuming high levels of saturated fats than in those consuming relatively more polyunsaturated fats. The evidence is by no means conclusive. The role of many other factors, like 'stress', physical inactivity, overweight and hypertension complicate the problem. Present views, suggest that the total fat intake should not be excessive (30–35% of calories) in a prudent diet, and that essential fatty acids, mainly linoleic acid (a polyunsaturated fatty acid) should make up about 15–20%. Rich sources of linoleic acid are corn oil, safflower seed oil, sunflower seed oil, etc.

Carbohydrate

Starches and sugars make up most of our calories, and foods rich in these also contain valuable amounts of minerals and vitamins, with the exception of refined sugars like sucrose (table sugar) and refined starch, which are pure carbohydrate. About 4 Kcal. per gram ($\equiv 16kJ/gram$) is provided by carbohydrate, and in many diets (particularly in poorer countries) the proportion of calories from carbohydrate is excessively high. High carbohydrate-containing unrefined foods, like vegetables, cereals, beans, and fruit, in addition to providing energy, minerals and vitamins, also furnish fibre (roughage) in the form of hemicelluloses, pectins, gums and lignin, which aid in maintaining bowel function and may have other beneficial effects (The Nutrition Society Symposium Reprint No. 5, 1973).

Minerals

There are some eighteen minerals that are essential to the regulation and maintenance of body processes. A deficiency of any one of these can make a difference between well-being and weakness, between health and illness. Thus sodium, essential in body fluids and tissues, is found in table salt and almost all foods; and potassium found in vegetables and fruit and to some extent in fish, meat, milk and coffee is required for healthy muscles and nerves. Calcium is necessary for teeth and bone structure, for blood clotting, and for normal muscle and nerve activity. Good sources of calcium are milk, cheese and green vegetables. Iron, the vital component of haemoglobin for oxygen transport from the lungs to the body cells is found in richest amounts in meat, especially liver, egg yolk, whole grain cereals and bread, leafy dark green vegetables, and dried fruit, peas and beans. There are other minerals necessary for health which are normally obtained in a balanced diet.

Vitamins

Vitamins are necessary for regulating many body processes. They include the fat soluble vitamins A,D,E,K, and the water soluble "B group" and C.

Vitamin A (Retinol). 5000 I.U. per day. Important for the development and maintenance of healthy skin and other epithelial tissues, particularly moist areas such as the front of the eyes, lining of the respiratory tract; and for integrity of night vision. Good food sources are liver and fish liver oils, kidney, milk fat, fortified margarine, egg yolk, and as the precursor, carotene, in yellow and dark-green leafy vegetables and fruit.

(Tocopherols) or Vitamin E. 30 mg. per day. Strong antioxidant which appears to protect red cells from haemolysis and prevents oxidation of unsaturated fatty acids and vitamin A in body tissues. Rich food sources are wheat germ, vegetable oils, green leafy vegetables, milk fat, egg yolk, nuts. Some gut synthesis may occur.

Vitamin D (Calciferol). 400 I.U. per day. Important for absorption and metabolism of calcium and phosphorus, normal bone and tooth formation and development. This vitamin is formed by the action of ultraviolet light on the skin and is obtained from fish liver oils, fortified margarine, butter and milk fat, liver, egg yolk, salmon, sardines and other fish.

Vitamin K (Phylloquinone). Recommended daily dose not established, but possibly about 0.5G. This vitamin is necessary for the production of prothrombin and for normal blood clotting. Good food sources are green leafy vegetables, tomatoes, cauliflower, wheat bran, liver, vegetable oils. Normal gut synthesis of the vitamin occurs.

Vitamin B1 (Thiamin). 0.4mg./1000Kcal./day. Essential for the enzyme, co-carboxylase, of carbohydrate metabolism, for normal appetite, digestion, and activity of nervous tissue. Good food sources are yeast, whole grain and enriched cereals, wheat germ, bread, legumes, potatoes, pork, liver, organ meats. Some gut synthesis occurs.

Vitamin B2 (Riboflavin). 0.6 mg./1000 Kcal./day. Necessary for ion transport in body and a co-enzyme in metabolism, for health of eyes, and for prevention of fissures at corners of mouth, nose and ears, eye irritation and photophobia. Found in yeast, green leafy vegetables, enriched cereals and bread, eggs, milk, dairy foods and organ meats.

Nicotinic acid (Niacin). 7 mg./1000 Kcal./day. As part of enzyme systems aids hydrogen ion transport and is involved in carbohydrate and amino acid metabolism. Prevents nervous depression and neuritis. Good food sources are yeast, cereal grains, bread, legumes, nuts, eggs, milk, liver and meat, poultry and fish.

Vitamin B6 (Pyridoxine). 2mg./day. Acts as a co-enzyme and is important for amino acid and essential fatty acid metabolism. Prevents hypochromic anaemia, certain types of dermatitis, mucous membrane lesions and peripheral neuritis. Good food sources are yeast, wheat germ, cereals, legumes, egg yolk, milk, liver and other meats.

Pantothenic acid. About 10mg./day. This vitamin forms part of coenzyme A and is involved in the metabolism of many vital body substances and in the metabolism of carbohydrate, fat, and protein. It is widely distributed in plant and animal foods, yeast, wheat germ, liver, salmon, etc.

Biotin. About 250 micrograms/day. A co-enzyme in metabolism of fat and amino acids, found in yeast, and most vegetables like mushrooms, tomatoes, fruit like bananas, grapefruit, watermelon, strawberries, and in milk, meat, egg yolk, nuts, etc.; gut synthesis occurs to some extent.

Folic acid (Pteroylmonoglutamic acid). About 0.1 mg./day. Involved in nucleic acid and fat metabolism, a co-enzyme, important for red cell maturation. Rich food sources are green leafy vegetables, wheat, dry beans, lentils, asparagus, broccoli, yeast, liver, organ meat, lean beef, eggs; gut synthesis occurs.

Vitamin B12 (Cyanocobalamin). About 5 micrograms/day. Important for metabolism of fat, nucleic acid, nervous system, and red cell formation. Only found in animal products so deficiency of this vitamin is often found in pure vegetarians. Good food sources are liver, kidney, meat, fish, eggs, milk and dairy produce. Some gut synthesis may occur.

Vitamin C (Ascorbic acid). About 20mg./1000Kcal. This vitamin acts as a co-enzyme in amino acid metabolism, is essential for hydroxylation reactions, for intercellular substance, and connective tissue and capillary integrity, for wound healing, steroid hormone synthesis, and reduces liability to certain inflammatory reactions and infections. Good food sources are fresh citrus fruits, strawberries, black currants, cherries, pineapple, tomatoes, melons, rose hips, peppers, greens, raw cabbage, potatoes, etc. Because of its rapid rate of oxidation, particularly in the presence of moisture, food losses of this vitamin occur readily.

Water. In a temperate climate and normal humidity, a moderately active man requires about 2½ litres of fluid daily (about 1ml./Kcal. food energy). This is usually obtained as one litre or so of water or beverage consumed, and about one and a half litres from preformed water in foodstuffs and metabolic water formed from fat, carbohydrate and protein. Some 60% of the body is made up of water necessary for a variety of structural, physiological and biochemical processes in the body. Normally, the total volume of body water is maintained within 0.3% of bodyweight. The sensation of thirst is stimulated when the total body water content decreases about 1%, and we drink to replace the lost fluid. However, in severe heat, strenuous exercise with excessive sweat loss, and in dry atmospheres and high altitude, water losses from the body may be excessive and the sensation of thirst may not keep pace with body water losses. In these conditions it may be necessary to deliberately increase fluid intake to avoid dehydration, tissue damage and excretory failure.

The Balanced Diet

A simple and widely used system for ensuring a balanced diet is the 'basic four' diet plan. This allows flexibility for seasonal, geographic and budgetary considerations and provides for the practical selection of the essential nutrients chosen from a variety of food stuffs. *Every day,* the individual should have at least *one item* from *each* of the following food groups:

Milk Group
2 or more cups of milk (or skim milk, evaporated milk, dry milk, butter milk or yoghurt); 1 oz. cheese or 1 serving of ice cream may be substituted for a cup of milk.

Meat Group

Twice daily, every one should have 2 or 3 ozs. meat of any kind, or poultry, or fish, or 2 eggs, or 1 cup dried beans, lentils, dried peas, or nuts, or 4 table-spoonfuls peanut butter.

Vegetable-Fruit Group

Every day, the individual should have 4 or more servings of vegetables and fruit. 1 serving should be a citrus fruit, or strawberries, tomatoes, melons, or other fruit rich in vitamin C, and every other day each person should have one serving of a dark green or yellow vegetable or fruit.

Bread-Cereal Group

Every day, the individual should have 4 or more servings of any of the following: (count as a serving 1 slice of bread, or 1 oz. ready to eat cereal, or ½ cup cooked cereal, or corn meal, or rice, macaroni, noodles, etc.).

The above plan provides for our basic metabolic needs, and for the essential nutrients. Other energy yielding foods, like sugar, sweets, butter, margarine, alcoholic drinks, fats and oils may be used to make up the calories for extra energy requirements.

Appetite and Food intake

In a normal man of fairly constant bodyweight and with readily available food supplies, the balance between energy intake from food and overall energy expenditure from the body is regulated with remarkable accuracy over long periods of time. This homeostatic regulation is controlled by the central nervous system, which monitors the feedback of information on body energy stores, energy utilisation for work and body temperature maintenance, and adjusts food intake to meet these varying energy requirements. It has been experimentally demonstrated that the co-ordinated activity of the lateral ('feeding centre') and ventromedial ('satiety centre') areas of the hypothalamus together with the neocortex, limbic system and other parts of the central nervous system, integrates the incoming information and via the sensations of hunger, appetite and satiety, initiates the 'drive' to eat and controls feeding behaviour and total food intake. Various theories have been proposed to explain the nature and mode of action of the 'signals' which affect the central regulation of food intake (Table 2). The appetite regulating system of a normal person is so efficient, that he eats just sufficient food without conscious effort, to maintain his bodyweight, and meet his basal metabolic and physical energy requirements. However, the 'stress' of severe physical activity, hypoxia, drastic environmental temperature change, as well as emotional, psychological, cultural, religious, social and economic factors, may exert profound effects on appetite. In addition, pathological conditions, various drugs, toxins and other deleterious agents may affect appetite, food intake and food preferences (Pawan, 1974). An unexplained fact of considerable interest is the remarkable ability of the indigenous populations in certain geographic areas to maintain apparently reasonable health and vigour on diets which would be quite inadequate for most persons from this country. The effects of mental and physical training, genetics, and environmental adaptation on nutritional requirements, efficiency of energy utilization, and physical performance, are complex and important areas for investigation.

The Mountaineer: Some Nutritional Suggestions and Recommendations

In addition to being healthy and fit, the mountaineer must be able to perform skilled and controlled movements with speed, coordination, repetition, ease and without fatigue, often in severe cold, hypoxic atmospheres, and dangerous conditions. His training, technical skill and equipment are invaluable, but diet is of paramount importance in helping him to achieve optimal bodyweight, nutritional status and mental and physical alertness. Throughout history, athletes have paid a great deal of attention to nutrition. The mountaineer is no exception.

Protein

It is now generally accepted that during muscular activity protein combustion is no greater than at rest, provided the energy supply from other sources, i.e. carbohydrate, fat and alcohol, is adequate (Pettenkofer & Voit, 1866; Hedman, 1957; Astrand & Rodahl, 1970). However, during training, particularly for 'music building', athletes from the time of the ancient Greeks (Harris, 1966) have been taking extra protein of high biological value (meat, fish, eggs, milk, cheese) in the belief that it improves their performance. Some authorities (Yoshimura, 1961) recommend high protein diets if heavy work is involved. The mountaineer should certainly have an adequate supply of protein in his diet, since the 'stress' of vigorous exercise and hypoxia produces some increase in adrenocortical activity (Moncloa, Velasco, & Beteta, 1968), thyroid secretion (Surks, 1966), proteinuria (Poortmans & Vankerchove, 1962) and increased needs for synthesis of haemoglobin, myoglobin, and various enzymes (Holloszy, Oscai, Don & Mole, 1970; Pernow & Saltin, 1971), all of which make extra demands on body protein stores. It is of interest to note that post-exercise proteinuria has been shown to decrease after training for several weeks (Cantone & Cerretelli, 1960). A protein intake of about 1 G./Kg. (i.e. 15% of the total caloric intake, and should be protein of high biological value) is recommended.

53

Carbohydrate and fat

Experimental studies of Christensen & Hansen (1939), Bergstrom, Hermansen, Hultman and Saltin (1967), Astrand & Rodahl (1970) and others, have demonstrated that a low carbohydrate diet plus vigorous physical exercise training for 3 or 4 days followed by a very high carbohydrate diet plus rest for three days immediately preceding a lengthy and severe athletic competition, produces a marked increase in muscle and liver glycogen stores which enables the athlete to perform heavy exercise for longer periods of time than if he had been having a normal proportioned diet. Dietary manipulation of dietary fat and carbohydrate has assumed great importance in modern athletics (Bergstrom & Hultman, 1972). There have also been suggestions that liquid glucose preparations, ingested during prolonged physical activity, may improve physical performance (Greene & Thomas, 1972; Consolazio & Johnson, 1972; Muckle, 1973; Brooke, 1973; Johnson & Rennie, 1974). Of particular interest to mountaineers is the monosaccharide sugar, fructose (laevulose), which occurs in high concentration (40%) in honey. This sugar has been shown to be a more efficient energy substrate at high altitude than at sea level (Reynafarje, Oyola, Cheesman, Marticorena & Jimenez, 1969). Details of the metabolism and usefulness of fructose has been recently reviewed (Pawan, 1973). In mountaineering, it is advisable to increase the percentage of carbohydrate and reduce the percentage of fat in the diet, i.e., to employ a diet providing about 55 to 60% of the calories as carbohydrate and about 25 to 30% of the calories as fat. This would tend to meet the craving for sweets and honey frequently felt at altitude. The high carbohydrate diet would also reduce the onset and severity of mountain sickness and improve physical performance and mental efficiency (Pugh & Ward, 1956; Van Liere, 1964; Cain & Dunn, 1966; Consolazio, Matoush, Johnson, Krzywicki, Daws & Isaac, 1969).

Another interesting nutritional aspect of mountaineering is the effects of high altitude, hypoxia, cold and physical activity producing increased lipolysis, mobilisation, and reduction of body fat stores and body weight, with increased levels of circulating free fatty acids and glycerol which enter the metabolic energy mixture and are used as a substrate by the muscle tissues (McElroy & Spitzer, 1961; Pugh, 1962; Gill & Pugh, 1964; Uspenskii & Chou-su, 1964; Hanson & Johnson, 1965; Masoro, 1966; Surks, Chinn & Matoush, 1966; Marger & Iampietro, 1966; Wilson, Laurell & Tibbling, 1969). This mobilisation of body fat stores is more rapid in well-trained than in untrained less-fit individuals (Issekutz, Miller, Paul & Rodahl, 1965; Carlson, Ekelund & Oro, 1963; Havel, 1965; Mole, Oscal & Holloszy, 1971). These changes are caused by a variety of lipolytic hormones whose secretion is increased (Pawan, 1971). Hypoxia may cause an increase in the basal metabolic rate (Chinn & Hannon, 1969), calorie intake reduction from anorexia and high altitude malabsorption (Pittman & Cohen, 1964), all of which may be involved in the loss of body fat at high altitudes.

Minerals

If excessive sweating and water loss occurs the importance of sodium and extra fluid are obvious. But high altitude can itself, via aldosterone changes and urinary losses, cause increased losses in sodium and increased urinary sodium: potassium ratios (Williams, 1966).

A normal intake of most of the other minerals appears adequate, with the possible exception of iron. At high altitude with intensive energy expenditure, the requirements for this mineral for synthesis of haemoglobin, myoglobin, metalloproteins and iron-containing enzymes are increased. The mountaineer should, therefore, have a sufficiency of this mineral, and this may be ensured by increasing his intake of substances which will facilitate iron absorption from the gut, such as ascorbic acid (Hegsted, Finch & Kinney, 1952), and fructose (Davis & Deller, 1967; Brodan, Brodanova, Kuhn, Kordac & Valek, 1967).

Vitamins

It would be prudent for the mountaineer to increase his intake of vitamin A for added protection to skin and epithelial tissues, such as the front of the eyes and lining of the respiratory tract. There have also been reports of high doses of this vitamin protecting against sunburn.

According to some authors, extra vitamin E is advisable in strenuous physical activities and various 'stress' conditions, as well as at high altitude (Cureton, 1954 and 1971; Prokop, 1960; Gounelle de Pontanel & Astier-Dumas, 1974), as it may help to reduce susceptability to lack of oxygen and decrease post-exercise 'oxygen debt'. It is also desirable to have extra vitamins of the B group and ascorbic acid.

Alcohol

Moderate amounts of alcohol (ethanol) are permitted for those who wish it, as this may have some psychological advantage in easing tension. Alcohol can provide some 7 Kcal. per gram. when metabolised, is helpful in small amounts in improving appetite and overcoming anorexia, and does help the absorption of iron. However, it should not be consumed prior to cold exposure, because of its peripheral vasodilating effects which may greatly increase heat loss, but it should be taken indoors or when reentering a warm tent, where its induction of a feeling of warmth may be of value. It should also be remembered that in the absence of food, e.g. after an overnight fast, a small amount of alcohol may in some individuals produce a marked fall in blood sugar. Alcohol also inhibits gluconeo-genesis from various precursors, and, following a bout of exercise, a moderate amount of alcohol may precipate a fall in blood glucose of sufficient severity to prevent the maintenance of body temperature in a moderately cold environment.

Further details of the nutritional and metabolic aspects of alcohol have been reviewed (Pawan, 1970 and 1972).

Finally, if one is travelling by air to a far distant country, it is important to have foods that one is accustomed to, at the right time and with proper hygienic safeguards, and to be careful with the water supply, including ice used in drinks. One should also remember that the cabin pressure in an air liner is equivalent to about 6500 ft. (2000 metres) altitude with low humidity. This inevitably causes excess water loss on long flights with symptoms of tiredness which may affect performance for a few days. Liberal fluid consumption during long flights should be advantageous.

References

Astrand, P.O. & Rodahl, K. (1970). Textbook of Work Physiology, *McGraw-Hill, N.Y.*

Bergstrom, J., Hermansen, L., Hultman, E. & Saltin, B. (1967). *Acta physiol. Scand., 71,* 140.

Bergstrom, J. & Hultman, E. (1972). *J. Amer. Med. Assoc., 221,* 999.

Brodan, V., Brodanova, M., Kuhn, E., Kordac, V. & Valek, J. (1967). *Nutrio et Dieta, 9,* 263.

Brooke, J.D. (1973) 'Carbohydrates & Human Performance', in 'Molecular Structure and Function of Food Carbohydrate', Editors: G.G. Birch & L.F. Green, *Applied Science Publications Ltd., London,* pages 235–261.

Cain, S.M. & Dunn, J.E. (1966), *J. Appl. Physiol. 21,* 1195.

Cantone, A. & Cerretelli, P. (1960). *Int. Z. angew. Physiol. einschl. Arbeitsphysiol., 18,* 324.

Carlson, L.A., Ekelund, L. & Oro, L. (1963). *J. Lab. Clin. Med. 61,* 724.

Chinn, K.S.K. & Hannon, J.P. (1969). *Fed. Proc., 28,* 944.

Christensen, E.H. & Hansen, O. (1939). *Scand. Arch. Physiol. 81,* 137.

Consolazio, C.F., & Johnson, H.L. (1972), *Amer. J. Clin. Nutrition, 25,* 85.

Consolazio, C.F., Matoush, L.O., Johnson, H.L., Krzywicki, H.J., Daws, T.A. & Isaac, G.J. (1969). *Fed. Proc. 28,* 937.

Cureton, T.K. (1954). *Amer. J. Physiol. 179,* 628.

Cureton, T.K. (1972). 'The Physiological effects of wheat germ oil on humans in exercise'., *Charles C. Thomas, Springfield, Illinois, U.S.A.*

Davis, P.S. & Deller, D.J. (1967). *Gut, 8,* 200.

Department of Health & Social Security (1969). 'Recommended Intakes of Nutrients for the United Kingdom.' Reports on Public Health and Medical Subjects. No. 120. *H.M. Stationery Office, London.*

Gill, M.B. & Pugh, L.G.C.E. (1964). *J. Appl. Physiol.,19,* 949.

Gounelle de Pontanel, H. & Astier-Dumas, M. (1974). *Annales d'hygiene de Langue Francais. Med. et Nutr. 10,* 251.

Green, L.F. & Thomas, V. (1972). *Proc. Nutr. Soc., 31,* 5A.

Hanson, P.G. & Johnson, R.E. (1965). *J. Appl. Physiol., 20,* 56.

Harris, H.A. (1966). *Proc. Nutr. Soc., 25,* 87.

Havel, R.J. (1965). *Annals. N.Y. Acad. Sci., 131,* 91.

Hedman, R. (1957). *Acta Physiol. Scand., 40,* 305.

Hegsted, D.M., Finch, C.A. & Kinney, T.D. (1952). *J. exp. Med., 69,* 115.

Holloszy, J.O., Oscai, L.B., Don, I.J. & Mole, P.A. (1970). *Biochem. Biophys. Res. Comm.*, *40*, 1368.

Issekutz, B., Miller, H.J., Paul, P. & Rodahl, K. (1965). *J. Appl. Physiol.*, *20*, 293.

Johnson, R. & Rennie, M. (1974). *New Scientist*, *64*, 585.

McElroy, W.T., & Spitzer, J.J. (1961). *J. Appl. Physiol.*, *16*, 760.

Marger, M. & Iampietro, P.F. (1966). *Metabolism*, *15*, 9.

Masoro, E.J. (1966). *Physiol. Rev. 46*, 67.

Mole, P.A., Oscai, L.B. & Holloszy, J.O. (1971). *J. Clin. Investigation, 50*, 2323.

Moncloa, F., Velasco, I. & Beteta, L. (1968). *J. clin. Endoc. Metab.*, *28*, 379.

Muckle, D.S. (1973). *Brit. J. Sports Med.*, *7*, 340.

Nutrition Society (1973). Symposium Reprint No. 5. 'Fibre in Human Nutrition', *The Nutrition Society, London.*

Pawan, G.L.S. (1970). *Nutrition, London, 24*, 77.

Pawan, G.L.S. (1971). *Brit. J. Hospital Med.*, *5*, 686.

Pawan, G.L.S. (1972). *Proc. Nutr. Soc.*, *31*, 83.

Pawan, G.L.S. (1973). 'Fructose' in 'Molecular Structure and Function of Food Carbohydrate', Editors: G.G. Birch & L.F. Green, *Applied Science Publications Ltd., London,* Pages 65–80.

Pawan, G.L.S. (1974). *Proc. Nutr. Soc.*, *33*, 239.

Pernow, B. & Saltin, B. (1971). 'Muscle metabolism during exercise', *Plenum, N.Y.*

Pettenkofer, M. & Voit, C. (1866). *Z. Biol.*, *2*, 459.

Pittman, J.G. & Cohen, P. (1964). *New Engl. J. Med.*, *271*, 453.

Poortmans, J. & Vankerchove, E. (1962). *Clin. Chim. Acta 7*, 229.

Prokop, L. (1960). *Sportarztl. Prax.*, *1*, 19.

Pugh, L.G.C.E. (1962), *Brit. Med. J.*, *ii*, 621.

Pugh, L.G.C.E. & Ward, M.P. (1956). *Lancet, ii*, 1115.

Reynafarje, B., Oyola, L., Cheesman, R., Marticorena, E. & Jimenez, S. (1969). *Amer. J. Physiol.*, *216*, 1542.

Surks, M.I. (1966). *J. clin. Invest.*, *45*, 1442.

Surks, M.I., Chinn, K.S.K., & Matoush, L.O. (1966). *J. Appl. Physiol.*, *21*, 1741.

Uspenskii, V.I. & Chou-Su, I. (1964). *Fed. Proc.*, *23*, *Trans. Suppl.* T939.

Van Liere, E.J. (1964). *Arch. Int. Med.*, *113*, 418.

Wilson, O., Laurell, S., Tibbling, G. (1969). *Fed. Proc.*, *28*, 1209.

Williams, E.S. (1966). *Proc. Roy. Soc., London, Series B, 165*, 266.

Yoshimura, H. (1961). *Fed. Proc.*, *20*, Part 3, 103. Suppl. 7.

Comparison of Body Composition and Energy Stores of a normal well-nourished 70Kg. (11 stone) man and an Obese man 145Kg. (23 stone).

	70 Kg. man	145 Kg. obese man
WATER	42 Kg. 60% Bodyweight	51 Kg. 35% Bodyweight
SOLIDS	28 Kg. 40% Bodyweight	94 Kg. 65% Bodyweight
FAT (adipose tissue)	15 Kg. 135000 Kcal.	80 Kg. 720000 Kcal.
PROTEIN (mainly muscle)	6 Kg. 24000 Kcal.	8 Kg. 32000 Kcal.
GLYCOGEN (muscle & liver)	0.19Kg. 760 Kcal.	0.23Kg. 920 Kcal.
GLUCOSE (extracellular fluid)	0.02 Kg. 80 Kcal.	0.025 Kg. 100 Kcal.
TOTAL	159840 Kcal.	753020 Kcal.

Table 1. (modified from G.L.S. Pawan (1971), Brit. J. Hospital Med., 5, 686)

Theories on the control of food intake: various factors may affect 'appetite' by modifying the nature and intensity of the 'signals'.

Theory	Origin of signals to the Central Nervous System	Reference
Gastrointestinal	Visual, olfactory, oral, pharyngeal Gastric distention, contraction, Osmolarity	Jacobs & Sharma (1969) Cannon & Washburn (1912) Smith (1966)
Thermostatic	Peripheral and Central heat monitors	Brobeck (1948)
Glucostatic	Specific receptors for glucose	Mayer (1953); Novin VanderWeele & Rezek (1973)
Lipostatic	Innervation of fat tissue Concentration of circulating metabolites: Progesterone? Prostaglandin?	Kennedy (1953) Hervey (1971) Baile, Simpson, Bean, McLaughlin & Jacobs (1973)
Amino acid pattern	Extracellular amino acids	Mellinkoff (1957)
Hypothalamic alpha and beta-adrenergic receptors	Resultant effect of agonists and antagonists	Liebowitz (1971)

Table 2. (after G.L.S. Pawan (1974). Proc. Nutr. Soc., *33*, 239)

Discussion

Prof. Williams. Would Dr. Pawan advise us on the peculiar ideas which people have about vitamins. Some we need to take and some we can forget about. Would he give us guidance?

Dr. Pawan. We can store vitamins in the body to guard against deficiency. Vitamin deficiency in two or three months on an expedition is very very unlikely provided one had a reasonable diet containing a sufficiency before departure.

Water soluble vitamins, especially C, are important, and it would perhaps be prudent for the mountaineer if he were to be away for a long time to take the B complex and Ascorbic acid (vitamin C) with him.

Dr. C. S. Houston. Some people think that you need your amino acids not just in the right proportion but in the same meal.

Dr. Pawan. There are 22 amino-acids in the body. Eight of these we cannot make. For synthesis we need a supply of all amino-acids at the same time. The same applies for carbohydrates. We get these most from animal proteins (meat, fresh eggs, etc.). Most vegetables, while they have *some* amino-acids, lack one, or may be more. So if we only took one vegetable we would get a diet lacking one or more essential amino-acids. We need to eat a variety of vegetables at the same meal in order to get our full complement of amino-acids.

Dr. Houston. So the types of vegetable are more important than eating vegetables.

Dr. Pawan. Good advice is to eat a variety of mixed foods at all times.

Dr. Houston. Is it possible to supplement a diet with specific amino-acids rather than just eating vegetables?

Dr. Pawan. Yes, this is what they have done with texturised proteins. They add the amino-acids that are lacking. Then you just add water.

A contributor asked about Lucozade.

Dr. Pawan. Lucozade analysis: Lucozade contains as much caffeine as a strong cup of coffee.

Dr. Catherine MacInnes. If you are going to put a high concentration of glucose into a dehydrated person are you not in danger of decreasing the blood volume?

Dr. Pawan. Agreed.

Prof. Odell. What is the significance of vitamin K?

Dr. Pawan. It has anti-haemorrhagic properties. You normally get enough by eating vegetables but pregnant women may need treatment with it against haemorrhages. You are unlikely to get a deficiency of it on an expedition lasting a few months.

Mr. Waller. Is there a significant relation between nutrition and the onset of cramp?

Dr. Pawan. Yes. This is ascribable to sodium loss. It occurs more in hot climates. A fall in ionised calcium in the blood can also cause it.

Dr. Leuthold. On the subject of fructose. We made a list of preferred nutrients. Honey ranked the highest.

Dr. Pawan. Do mountaineers take salt tablets with them in the mountains?

Major Fleming. No.

Dr. Rennie. The quickest way to get cramp is to reduce the water in the body — not the salt.

Dr. Leuthold. Mountaineers have asked us if they need to take minerals in view of the fact that they collect water from the snow. The answer which we have given is No.

Dr. Houston. Is there any good data to support the need for trace elements? (Cobalt — zinc — manganese).

Dr. Pawan. Yes, they are very important, but the likelihood of a mountaineer on a balanced pre-expedition diet getting a deficiency while on an expedition is very small. And it is very difficult to find a diet which *is* deficient in these trace elements.

Prof. Williams. As an illustration take the trace element iodine. Everybody here has two years of iodine repletion. It is possible that we have cobalt etc., stores as well.

Practical Problems of Nutrition

H. W. TILMAN

As I have not visited the Himalayas since 1951 my thoughts on feeding are a bit old-fashioned. I could speak with more authority on victualling a small boat for a long voyage which I have done every year for the last twenty years.

When a party increases its numbers until it is labelled an expedition the man responsible for the food will be obliged to steer a middle course between extreme types. On the one hand are the men — I quote Carlyle — "whose principal enjoyment is their dinner and who watch the sun rise with no other hope than that they shall fill their bellies before it sets"; and on the other the austere type, the genuine travellers who, according to the Spanish proverb, "should have the back of an ass to bear all and the mouth of a hog to eat whatever is set before him." He has also to bear in mind whether it is one of those sponsored expeditions where someone kindly foots all the bills or whether those taking part are paying for their pleasure. The latter is commendable but the snag is that those who pay the piper expect to call the tune. Which is why that on these voyages of mine I find it best to do all the paying, for otherwise the crew might consider themselves paying passengers, fully entitled to grumble and grouse about what they have to eat.

Up to say 23000 ft. the choice of what to take is wide enough unless one is obliged to travel light when selection becomes all-important. But the technique of travelling light favoured by Shipton and I in the distant past need not mean semi-starvation. Because we once had to live for a few days on tree mushrooms and bamboo shoots there is a general and mistaken impression that this was our normal diet, eked out with liberal doses of fresh air, on which, thanks to a yogi-like training, we managed to thrive and expected everyone else to do the same. Nothing could be further from the truth. Like Dr. Johnson we minded our bellies very strenuously. "For I take it,", says the sage, "that he who will not mind his belly will scarcely mind anything else."

The more restricted a diet the more need there is for care in its selection. For normal men a ration of about 2 lbs. a day is about right and the whole art lies in getting value for weight. On Polar expeditions, where conditions are more severe, the work as hard, and the period more prolonged, the sledging ration varies from 25 to 33 ozs. and it is far simpler and on the face of it less appetising than the food taken on Himalayan expeditions. The difference is that there are no altitude problems and the men are hungry. Watkins wrote of his 1930 Greenland party: 'We soon found that the ration of 39 ozs. was more than enough for men travelling 20 and 30 miles a day at low temperatures at a height of 8000 ft. and towards the end we reduced the ration by one-third so that the total amount was 23 ozs. This was found ample for normal sledging work." Martin Lindsay on the other hand wrote: "We found ourselves ravenously hungry on 26 ozs. a day. Were this journey (the crossing of the Greenland ice-cap) to be done again I should increase the ration to 32 ozs."

If 2 lbs a day is adequate for this kind of work it is enough for Himalayan parties and on this allowance estimates are usually based. One assumes that any traveller – that is one who moves by his own exertions – and, of course, all mountaineers, are concerned about weight and economy of food without making a fetish of it. Viewed in this light jam, for example, is not worth carrying; the only useful part of it is the sugar, so that a 1 lb tin, weighing probably 19 ozs. gross, will contain less than half that weight of useful food. From a quarter to a fifth of the weight of all tinned food is provided by the tin, and other obvious reasons for avoiding it as far as possible are cost, lack of freshness, and sameness. Food picked up locally wherever possible has therefore the advantage of freshness and saves both money and transport. The proportions of food to be taken can be allocated roughly to 30% protein, 10% fats, and 60% carbohydrates, dividing the last item into half cereals and half sugar. Coarse local flour (atta) is better value than white flour, unpolished rice than polished, sugar from a local mill (jaggery in India, gur in Africa) better than refined sugar. This is as good as home-made fudge but there is so much moisture in it that the main sugar supply must be white. Of this ½ lb. a man a day is none too much.

Where transport is a cut-and-dried affair – as for example to Everest – weight has not to be regarded so rigorously as on a difficult journey; there is nothing like having to carry or pull your own loads for teaching sense in this respect. I have been looking up what we took to Everest in '38 and find we did ourselves ‹ pretty well, our diet including much that was not really necessary, much that – as the sage said of marriage – was rather to be permitted than approved. Bacon, ham, cheese, butter, and pemmican figure largely. Eggs could be got on the march, and by eggs I mean half a dozen or so a man, fewer are not much good, but for use on the mountain we had six hundred eggs preserved in water-glass, so that every morning, even on the North Col, we had the English breakfast fetish of bacon and eggs. As far as Camp III (21500 ft.) we ate normal food like meat, potatoes, rice, lentils, the meat being either freshly killed sheep or yak, or failing that dried mutton which in Tibet is a staple commodity. For this sort of food one needs a pressure cooker without which it would take too long owing to the low temperature at which water boils. At 20000 ft. it is only 180°F. instead of 212°F. With dried yeast we made bread from the local atta, quite unlike the flaccid product of starch and chemicals sold as bread in this country. The aforesaid meagre diet which might be all very well for ascetics, was eked out with milk, porridge, jam, honey, dried fruits, sweets, chocolate, sugar, glucose, dripping, biscuits, soups. Nevertheless some of the party were mightily relieved to find at Rongbuk quantities of stores left by the 1936 party, and thought that this windfall, consisting mainly of nourishing foods like jam, pickles, and liver extract, alone saved us from starvation.

It is above 23000 ft that the problem of what to eat becomes acute, especially if several days have to be spent at great heights. So far it has been found impossible to eat enough of any kind of food in such conditions, even the supposedly tempting luxuries beloved by what I call the 'quails in aspic' school of thought, for which the shelves of high-class grocers like Fortnum & Mason's have been ransacked. The pressure cooker has to be left behind, cooking is hardly on anyway beyond the boiling of water for tea or soup, and one is driven back upon preserved and processed foods out of tins and jars, so that the disinclination to eat anything that is already making itself felt becomes even stronger. Eating is then a distasteful duty rather than a pleasure, and whether food eaten in such circumstances is of any benefit at all is a question for physiologists.

It is this absence of hunger which makes the problem of high altitude feeding so different from that, say, in the Arctic, where the ration has only to be designed to maintain the bodily heat and energy of hard working men. There, concentrated foods rich in fat, such as pemmican, provide a solution which any dietician can work out, and there such foods can be eaten with gusto; but a way of maintaining the heat and energy of hard-working men who are not hungry, and to whom the thought of food is slightly nauseating, is less easily found. If you do succeed in getting outside a richly concentrated food like pemmican a great effort of will is required to keep it down — absolute quiescence in a prone position and a little sugar are useful aids. Eating a large mug of pemmican soup at 27200 ft, as Peter Lloyd and I did in '38 is, I think, an unparalleled feat and shows what can be done by dogged greed. For greed consists of eating when you have no desire to eat which is more or less the case anywhere above 23000 ft. Of two equal candidates for a place in an Everest party it might pay to take the greediest, overlooking his disgusting habits at low levels for the sake of his capacity to eat at higher.

Fluid intake is, of course, another deficiency and the trouble here is not lack of desire but the time consumed in melting and heating snow in sufficient quantities, though I believe that since the war great improvements have been made in the efficiency of heating stoves. The loss of weight and consequent weakness which invariably follows a stay at high altitudes is no doubt as much due to the lack of food as to the effort expended. More use, I think, might be made of eggs. They are not difficult to carry and can be easily cooked in a variety of ways or eaten raw. Dried egg is questionable. At sea I find it requires large quantities of Tabasco sauce to make it palatable. Other suggestions were sardines, dried bananas, pickled beef, kippers, cream cheese — suggestions that were made, be it noted, at Camp III and not at Camp VI where they would have to be eaten. The fact is that at those heights lying in a sleeping bag doing nothing is so pleasant that some show of resolution is required even to begin the simplest preparations for eating, entailing as they do the search for food amongst the bedding, spare clothes, boots, rope, oil, meths, candles, cameras, saucepans, and snow littering the tent floor.

The difficulty of eating at high altitudes was noted by Norton, that outstanding figure in the annals of Everest, in whose Horse Battery, by the way, I served for a short time in 1918 in France. Of 1924 he wrote: "There is no doubt that it is exceedingly difficult to hit on the right sort of food for high altitudes." He then lists that they had bully beef, tongue, sardines, pemmican, Ginger nuts, Plasmon biscuit, jams, butter scotch, peppermint, Force, Grape Nuts, spaghetti, cheese, crystallised fruits, Elvas plums, tea, cocoa, cafe au lait — and concludes, "Apart from these no varieties of food will be found necessary or for that matter palatable." In fact what Norton noted had been noted much earlier and at a much lower level. An early Victorian climber discussing the ascent of Mt. Blanc stated flatly; "Provisions are of no use, all that is needed is an umbrella and a scent bottle".

In 1953 what they called the Assault Ration sounds thinner and less sustaining than Norton's list, but then we don't know how much if any of that was actually eaten. They had rolled oats, milk powder, sugar, jam, sweet biscuits, mint bar, cheese, boiled sweets, salt, cocoa, tea, soup, lemonade powder. I have no experience of it but should have thought that using oxygen while climbing and sleeping would leave a man less exhausted and possibly with more appetite. It is proverbially difficult to blow and swallow at the same time but could not technicians devise a way of eating and breathing oxygen at the same time?

I have no time left for the question of pre-packed ration boxes which are common form nowadays even on the approach march. They certainly save the man in the field any need for thought or resourcefulness and they must bring home to the men who have to eat the contents that they are indeed on an expedition. Last year in Spitzbergen we met a Cambridge geological party who though at that moment were living in what was almost a town still ate out of ration boxes. Lifeboat biscuits had been their portion since their arrival and it did one good to see how they relished our bread. For high camps pre-packed boxes are certainly an advantage but apart from that I would rather be without them.

On the whole, travellers and mountaineers, when pursuing their vocations, should be in agreement with Thoreau, the great apostle of the simple life, who held that most of the luxuries and nearly all the so-called comforts of life are not only indispensable but are positively a hindrance to the *elevation* of mankind.

Discussion

Sqn. Ldr. Davies. (To Tilman). Did you take tea or coffee on expeditions? The Mountain Rescue people advise us to take coffee.

Mr. Tilman. I would take coffee if it were good. But I am a coffee expert having been involved in producing it in Kenya. I do not consider it possible to find good coffee and so I recommend tea every time!

Dr. Pawan had analysed the contents of a flask of coffee and of one of tea. The value of these stimulants is that they cause a mobilisation of fats.

Sir Jack Longland. Can anyone give the up-to-date view of acclimatisation and lack of appetite. We found appetite improved as we went higher.

Mr. Ward. A well acclimatised person is a hungry one.

Dr. Milledge. The longer we stayed at the Silver Hut the worse our appetites got. We tended to be worse in the mornings. We improved in the course of the day. This may be because at night you tend to be more hypoxic. Breakfast is the difficulty. We relished chapattis and foods like curries with good flavours.

Hypoxia: Some Experiences on Everest and elsewhere

N. E. ODELL

The early Everest expeditions of 1922 and 1924 were equipped with oxygen-breathing apparatus, which was based very largely on experimental work carried out in de-compression chambers, to simulate the low partial pressures of oxygen existing at very high altitudes. Prominent among these experimenters were Professor Sir Joseph Barcroft, Prof. J. S. Haldane, Dr. (later Prof. Sir Bryan) Matthews, Prof. G. Dreyer, Dr. A. M. Kellas, Sir Leonard Hill, Prof. Yandell Henderson (of Yale) and others, who gave useful advice based upon laboratory evidence or, in some cases, on actual high mountain ascents, as in the Andes and Himalaya. In the laboratory Barcroft, Douglas Kendal & Margaria had shown that at 170 mm. of pressure while breathing oxygen, man can step up 1000 ft. in an hour. This expended work consisted of stepping on to a box and down again. But 170 mm. is a much lower pressure than the top of Everest (230 mm.). Consequently it was clear that the feat of climbing to the highest altitudes was not impossible if oxygen could be got into the climbers' respiratory passages. Thus arose the problem of apparatus for a suitable supply of oxygen on the mountain, merely "an engineer's problem", as conceived by Barcroft.

In 1922 when the second Everest expedition* was first equipped with an oxygen apparatus, George Finch and Geoffrey Bruce, making full use of it from about 20,000 ft., reached an approximate altitude on the rocks of the north (Tibetan) face of 27,235 ft. But in spite of the oxygen they had suffered frostbite (Bruce severely), and on arrival at the base camp they were both quite exhausted. Preceding this attempt was that of the non-oxygen party, consisting of Mallory, Norton, Somervell and Morshead (part-way only). In spite of very difficult conditions of stormy wind and bitter cold, together with newly fallen snow, they managed to reach an altitude a little less, by 200 ft., than that attained by the oxygen party. It was Somervell's confirmed opinion that a future party would have a better chance of climbing Everest if oxygen were not

*'The Assault on Mount Everest, 1923. Brig. Gen. the Hon. C. G. Bruce et al.

67

used, since by so doing natural acclimatisation is prevented: a view-point stoutly opposed by Finch, who incidentally was by profession a chemist.

Consequently, by the time of the third Everest expedition of 1924* it was felt that the problem of oxygen was unproven, but that if a lighter apparatus could be devised, and sufficient porters be made available to carry up supplies, benefit might accrue from using it high on the mountain; at any rate medical opinion was in favour of its being available for clinical use, such as in cases of frost-bite. The present writer was appointed oxygen-officer, but was obliged to go off on geological duty in the oilfields of Persia during the winter just prior to the expedition. Then there was delay in the oxygen apparatus being despatched from England, and when it reached us serious defects and leakages were found, which were difficult to rectify during the wintry march across Tibet and at the Base camp. While this work was proceeding, sahibs and porters were carrying up loads to equip and stock the long line of camps that had to be established up the glaciers and on to the mountain itself. It was, of course, this necessity entailing going up and down from base camp repeatedly that brought about a higher degree of acclimatisation in the party than had ever been attained previously in the Himalaya. Eventually, largely due to the skill of Irvine, three or four sets of oxygen apparatus became available later on in our operations, but too late to try to get the benefit that theoretically we should have been getting if using it earlier. However, after the very remarkable attempt on the summit by Norton and Somervell, who reached an altitude of about 28,130 ft., entirely without an artificial supply of oxygen, Mallory decided to make one last attempt, with Irvine as his companion, and using oxygen at least for the last stages of the climb. I followed them up in support, and became engrossed in my geological observations, and then glancing up at the ridge above saw them silhouetted against the snow near what we called the First Step, at a range of about 800 yards. What happened to them later we may never know, but it is possible that they may have reached the summit, although behind their own schedule as suggested by Mallory. But I think that it should be of interest to mention that in the interval of 50 years since Mallory and Irvine disappeared there have been several psychic messages purporting to come from one or other of them and each claiming success. I shall only mention one, from Irvine, that came to me last year from a friend in Shetland. Briefly it was that they both got to the summit, but that an accident occurred on their descent. The editor of the Alpine Journal has agreed to put my report, without comment, in the next (1975) Journal. Many will, of course, disbelieve it. Others who are not psychic nor spiritualists may have open minds on these matters and on such reports. I may mention, however, that I found my friend, Howard Somervell, that wide-ranging thinker and accomplished artist, was extremely interested, and considered

*The Fight for Everest, 1924. Lt. Col. E.F. Norton, et al.

Irvine's message regarding what had happened as most plausible. I myself reserve an open mind on it, which I believe should be the attitude of the consistent scientist!

In "The Fight for Everest 1924" I recounted my own physiological experiences on the mountain during the last stages of our operations in 1924. In the role of support to Mallory and Irvine, and during my search for them after their return was overdue, I found that I was able to climb, without using oxygen, to over 27,000 ft. on two occasions. Earlier, when our reconstituted oxygen sets had become available, Geoffrey Bruce and I had been unable to derive any benefit from the oxygen on an ascent from Camp III (21,000 ft) to the North Col (22,980 ft.), presumably due to our acclimatised condition. Later, above the Col, and out on the exposed face of the mountain, I experienced the same negative effect; although I carried an apparatus involving an extra burden of about 28 lbs, I could get no extra 'kick' from the oxygen when for a time it was turned on. All this I described in "The Fight for Everest" and elsewhere, and especially in my much later paper, written after the successful ascent of the mountain in 1953: "Reflections on Everest. Acclimatisation versus the Use of Oxygen on High Mountains" (Canadian Alpine Journal 1954 and also in N.Z. Alpine Journal).

Shipton's surprising conjecture. Although it seemed that I had demonstrated a high degree of acclimatisation, almost to the tune of Sir Jack Longland's remark that I was a 'freak' (!) 'lusus naturae', it may be amusing and perhaps not irrelevant to add that Eric Shipton in a lecture to the Royal Central Asian Society claimed that I was seriously unacclimatised! For as reported in the Society's Journal, Vol. XXV, April, 1938, p. 262 to illustrate the fact that "due to the altitude my brain was not functioning well", at about 26,000 ft. I excitedly collected a couple of fossils, and put them in my pocket, later when feeling hungry, he said, I took them out, bit them, and thinking they were frozen bread threw them away! "He did not remember", says Shipton, "until he got down that that was what had happened". As I later pointed out in a letter to the Society's Journal XXVI, April 1939, p. 366, I did not throw away so-called 'fossils', but brought them back for diagnosis; and later finding them to be an unusual form of "cone-in-cone" structure, I gave them with other geological specimens to the British Museum (Natural History) at South Kensington.

British Association Centenary Meeting, 1931. At this important meeting in London, presided over by General Smuts, Professor Barcroft, of Cambridge, read a paper to Section I. (Physiology) entitled "The limits placed by altitude to physical exercise". To this meeting he urged that Dr. Raymond Greene and myself should come. Greene had just returned from the ascent of Kamet (25,447 ft.) in the Kumaon Himalaya, and I had to be procured from an expedition in the mountains of Northern Labrador. This meeting raised a very interesting discussion, as well as much resulting correspondence in the pages of "Nature" during 1931 and 1932, particularly from Sir Leonard Hill, Prof. Rodolfa Margaria (of Turin), Prof. Yandell Henderson (of Yale), Dr. Greene, myself and others. As cited later by Dr. Greene in "Everest 1933", by Ruttledge, p. 251, a committee was formed as an outcome of the above discussion, and another and lighter oxygen apparatus was devised of 12 lbs. 12 oz. weight. But sundry differences of opinion still persisted among the pundits, especially on the question of 'open' versus 'closed circuit' apparatus, and even as to the real efficacy of oxygen as opposed to acclimatisation. Moreover, several of the climbers on the 1933 expedition were opposed to the use of even this improved and lighter apparatus since, as Greene relates, an ascent *without* oxygen was deemed much more sporting! But this same sentiment had been felt before, in 1922, when Mallory objected to Finch's rigid belief in the necessity for oxygen; and later, may be mentioned, Irvine's protest to me that he would rather attain the base of the final pyramid of Everest without oxygen than the summit depending on it! This was a signific- ant attitude in view of the circumstances of his last climb with Mallory, but it was one that tended to persist during the further pre-War attempts in 1936 and 1938; reliance on acclimatisation being paramount, at least up to 27,000 ft. or even more. However, as Charles Warren (our M.O. both these years) has des- cribed in the Alpine Journal LI., Nov. '39, No. 259, and elsewhere, we were provided in 1938 (as in 1936) with both experimental 'open' and 'closed circuit' type of apparatus; and our experiences with them varied considerably. Above the North Col (23,000 ft.) in 1938 Peter Lloyd tried out both sets, and experienced only partial benefit from the 'open' type, but almost 'suffocation' when using the other set! This experience of suffocation with 'closed circuit' apparatus is not unique, and Warren has commented on its drawbacks and puzzling character. He concludes, however, that "the theoretical advantages of the closed circuit type are outweighed by the disadvantages of its greater weight and increased complexity when compared with the open variety." ("Mountain sickness and the physiological problems of high altitude mountainnering". A.J. LI. Nov. 1939.)

Arising out of all these earlier experiences, it would seem unnecessary, nor will space permit, to recount such later findings as those from John Hunt's successful expedition of 1953. These are amply described and are easily accessible in his book "The Ascent of Everest". Suffice it to say that full recognition was given to the necessity for acclimatisation at more moderate altitudes before the climbing parties went high. Moreover, it was the second pair, Hillary and Tenzing, using an improved 'open' type of oxygen-set that were successful from a high bivouac, 'Ridge Camp'; while the first summit-contenders, Bourdillon and Evans, with a closed-circuit set, and starting from the South Col at 26,000 ft. could not get beyond the 'South Summit' (28,700 ft), mainly on account of difficulties with their breathing apparatus, particularly Evans' set.

Acclimatisation versus Deterioration. As far as the problem of acclimatisation is concerned and its ultimate high-altitude possibilities, it is worth-while recalling the outstanding case of the Bavarian mountaineers, under Dr. Paul Bauer's leadership, on Kangchenjunga in 1929 and 1931. On the north-east spur of that mountain, under extreme difficulties of climbing and the worst of monsoon conditions, they worked upwards for sixty-eight days to establish a long line of camps, and reached an altitude of about 26,000 ft. No oxygen was necessary nor was its want felt. (See "High Altitude and Oxygen", N.E. Odell: Himalayan Journal IV., 1932, with note by the editor.). In the light of such an achievement one can only feel that the remark of Drs. Pugh and Ward in the "Ascent of Everest" p. 270, by John Hunt, was premature: "The strain of going above 26,000 ft. is such that few can recover from it."

In my spoken contribution at the symposium I called attention also to the important showing of acclimatisation by the American party on K2 in 1953 under Dr. Charles Houston, my companion earlier (1936) on Nanda Devi. His party of eight climbed through very bad weather and without oxygen, and arrived in good condition to establish their Camp 8 at about 25,500 ft. They were held up there for eleven days by bad storms, and finally had to make a remarkable and successful retreat down the mountain, but with the tragic loss of one climber, Gilkey (the geologist), who was carried away by an avalanche. Dr. Houston declared afterwards that he saw no reason whatsoever, to change his opinion that the summit of K2 (28,250 ft.) is reachable by well-acclimatised men, without extra oxygen. And he added that he was reasonably confident that Everest would be climbed within the next generation without extra oxygen!

I may add here that on our Nanda Devi expedition in 1936 we were not equipped with oxygen, except with one set for clinical purposes (and that was lost accidentally in the Rishi Ganga on our way in); and Tilman and I did not feel the want of it during our climb to the summit of 25,640 ft.

The problem of acclimatisation versus deterioration is still with us and so far is indeterminate. On our descent from Everest in 1938 Dr. Warren was much puzzled by the paralysis developed by one of our young Sherpas, Pasang Shotia. The latter had carried manfully to Camp V. (25,800 ft.) and beyond, and then became completely paralysed down one side; he could not walk at all, and had to be carried and lowered with great difficulty the whole way down the face of the North Col and then on down the glacier. Warren has discussed whether the paralysis might not have been brought on by altitude; whether alterations in the blood due to acclimatisation, e.g. clotting in the vessels of the brain, because the blood has become more viscous, and so brought about such a serious condition, intermediate apparently between the benefits of acclimatisation and the ill-effects of deterioration. But Pasang's would seem to be a special case. Moreover, to the writer's knowledge there is no record of permanent physiological ill-effects being suffered by climbers, nor porters, as far as he knows, on Everest or other Himalayan expeditions; for although dilated hearts have sometimes resulted amongst those going high, they have always been sufficiently 'elastic' to return quickly to normal. Personally I may say that after Everest in 1924 (when aged 33), Nanda Devi in 1936 (aged 45), and Everest again in 1938 (aged 47), I had speedily experienced my normal fitness in general. Incidentally it is somewhat amusing to recall that in 1936, when Tilman and I were candidates for Ruttledge's party to Everest, we were both turned down as two ('too') old men! So we turned profitably to Nanda Devi! A factor in our ability, without distress, to reach the summit of the latter may well have been due to physiological tolerance of high altitude, acquired and retained from previous Himalayan expeditions. It is well known that this tolerance can persist over many years. In 1924 it was very noticeable that Mallory acclimatised quickest, due to his two previous visits; next were those who had been once previously, and slowest were the newcomers.

Finally, I feel compelled to take this opportunity to record what immense benefit personally I have derived from experience at high altitudes. As a schoolboy I was plagued with severe psoriasis extending from head to foot, and every kind of superficial treatment was tried on me from a large range of ointments to ultra-violet and X-rays etc., but without benefit. However, on holidays in the Alps and climbing to 10,000 ft., or less, this troublesome disease quickly left me, and did not return from some six months or so. But eventually at higher Himalayan altitudes it disappeared 'in a flash', and finally left me for good. Physicians, whom I have known, have seemed but partially interested in my case-history of psoriasis, but it is surely a pity that such an easy and pleasant 'cure' for this distressing disease should not be more widely known and recommended.

Discussion

Dr. Warren. How long did you spend at the High Camp on Everest?

Prof. Odell. I never spent a night at camp 7. We worked from 6, or indeed 5.

Sir Jack Longland. No oxygen at all was used in 1933. The same height was reached as that attained by Somervell and Mallory. I think that but for Everest's snowed up condition, Wyn-Harris and Smythe were physically capable of getting up without oxygen. (And, incidentally, in 1924 there was no Camp 7.)

Physiological Effects of Hypoxia

J. S. MILLEDGE

One of the problems for the climber at high altitude is lack of oxygen, or hypoxia. Not that there is a shortage of oxygen in the air at altitude, it still contains 21% oxygen, but it is present at a lower pressure than at sea level. The fall of pressure with altitude is curvilinear, being more rapid in the first 10,000 ft and by 18–19,000 ft the pressure is half than at sea level.

The effects of this reduction in oxygen pressure (pO_2) rate at which it is reduced. Aviation medicine is concerned with the effects of sudden hypoxia, as when an aircraft suddenly loses cabin pressure. Studies in decompression chambers are usually about these acute effects. Figure 1 shows the effect on man of being suddenly exposed to increasing altitude and is based on such studies.

As low as 4,000 ft, night vision, the most sensitive function in the body, is measurably affected. At 6,000 or 7,000 ft slight breathlessness on exertion may be detected and becomes more obvious at higher altitudes. At about 16,000 ft one may get feelings of tingling in the lips or fingers, feelings of unreality, and dizziness. Finally, from 20,000 ft or so unconsciousness descends with increasing speed until one has only about two minutes useful consciousness after sudden exposure to 29,000 ft – the height of Mount Everest.

By contrast, if one allows time in going up to altitude as should be the case in climbing expeditions, the body adjusts in a remarkable way and then the effects are those shown in Figure 2.

The earliest and always dominant symptom is that of breathlessness, which at first is only appreciated on exertion. It becomes noticeable at about 10,000 ft onwards and increases with increasing altitude. A line is shown for the ventilation at 900 kg. m. min. which is approximately the work rate which a climber adopts when climbing at his preferred rate. At sea level this requires a ventilation of around 50 litres per minute and this increases with altitude as shown until, by about 21,000 feet, 160 litres per minute ventilation is needed to sustain this work rate. Of course, long before this the climber has had to slow down and, indeed, at about 18,000 or 19,000 feet, continuous climbing, which is recommended normally in climbing in this country and the Alps, ceases to be possible. Above this altitude climbing has to be intermittent, with pauses to get one's breath and repay the oxygen debt. Indeed, Sherpas and other high altitude residents, particularly when load carrying, adopt this intermittent form of climbing from very much lower altitudes and for them it does seem to be the most efficient method. This is probably because when the climbing rate becomes very low a lot of energy is expended in merely holding one's balance between slow steps. Above about 17,000 feet breathlessness is noted at rest. The highest permanent habitation is also shown on Figure 2 at about 17,000 feet and it seems that above this altitude it is not possible to live indefinitely. Climbing with oxygen becomes worthwhile at about 23,000 feet — below this altitude, although oxygen does reduce the ventilation and make the climber feel more comfortable, the price paid in the extra weight makes it hardly worthwhile. The highest point climbed without oxygen is just over 28,000 feet, which was attained by four separate individuals on Everest in the pre-war period, and finally, the highest that I have been able to find for an acclimatised individual in a pressure chamber, remaining conscious, is 32,000 feet, which was achieved by an individual in Moracocha who, having acclimatised to 14,000 feet, entered the pressure chamber and went slowly up in simulated altitude to this height without loss of consciousness.

Comparing the differences between Figures 1 and 2, we have summarised the effect of acclimatisation. Indeed, it is really remarkable the way the body can adapt to the reduction in this most vital element — oxygen supply to the tissues.

Altitude acclimatisation. One way of classifying these changes, which was first produced by Barcroft, is by examining the various steps in the oxygen transport system of the body from outside air to the mixed venous blood which is close to the values for tissues in the body. This system is shown diagramatically in Figure 3, where the values for oxygen pressure (pO_2) at sea level and at 19,000 feet are shown.

Looking at the system at sea level first, we see the ambient pO_2 is about 160 mm Hg. As the air is warmed and wetted in the mouth and pharynx the O_2 is diluted with water vapour and its pressure drops to 150 mm Hg. Then, as we go down the airways to the alveoli, the fresh air mixes with gas already there from which oxygen has been removed and carbon dioxide added. Thus there is a drop of about 50 mm Hg to a pO_2 of 100 mm Hg.

The next drop from alveolar to arterial is sometimes called the diffusion gradient. Loss of oxygen pressure is due to gas exchange across the alveolar membranes from gas to blood, which entails a drop of about 6–10 mm Hg pressure.

Finally, the drop from arterial to mixed venous blood is again approximately 50 or 60 mm Hg and depends upon the oxygen carrying capacity of blood, the rate of blood flow through the body, and the metabolic needs of the body. Now, if we examine the lower line at altitude (Figure 3), it will be seen in general that the body makes attempts to reduce these gradients at every step. The ambient pO_2 is half that at sea level – about 80 mm Hg. The initial drop due to wetting of the inspired air cannot be reduced. It is a purely physical effect of diluting the oxygen with water vapour and we lose 10 mm Hg at altitude which, of course, represents a more important proportion of the total. The next step from expired to to alveolar is amenable to reduction and is one of the major points at which acclimatisation can help the individual. Breathing is initially stimulated by the effect of low oxygen on the carotid body – an organ closely associated with the carotid artery in the neck. Low oxygen pressure in arterial blood stimulates this organ, which has nervous connections with the respiratory centre in the brain and stimulates that to increase ventilation. However, in the unacclimatised individual, this stimulus is partly opposed by the loss of drive from carbon dioxide, which is washed out. Acclimatisation increases the sensititivy of the respiratory centre to carbon dioxide in a remarkable way. Normally at sea level the ventilation is controlled by the level of carbon dioxide. If the carbon dioxide level in the body increases, this is appreciated by receptors in the brain which stimulate the respiratory centre to increase the rate of breathing, thus bringing the carbon dioxide level back to normal. This mechanism has been investigated by giving subjects increasing amounts of carbon dioxide to breathe in the inspired air and observing the ventilation that is produced by this increased level of carbon dioxide mixtures and measuring the ventilation it is possible to construct a carbon dioxide response curve as shown by the line furthest right in Figure 4. If such an experiment is repeated, giving similar carbon dioxide mixtures but now with reduced oxygen, it is found that the line of the response curve steepens and in this way a family of response curves at varying oxygen levels can be produced, as shown in Figure 4 – the right hand 'fan'. The numbers at the end of each line indicate the pO_2 of that response line.

In the Silver Hut expedition we carried out such experiments on ourselves, initially in Oxford and later, after acclimatisation, in the Silver Hut, and our results are summarised in Figure 4. You see that the whole fan of CO_2 response lines is shifted to the left. At sea level this fan appears to originate at approximately 38 mm Hg pCO_2, whereas at altitude it has shifted to the left to about 23 mm Hg. In other words, the level at which the respiratory centre appears to respond to carbon dioxide has been reduced almost by half. The other change is that, having started to respond, the centre responds more briskly to any increment in carbon dioxide. We found that the effect of hypoxia on top of this carbon dioxide response had not been altered from the situation at sea level. This change in carbon dioxide response takes place over a period of a few days after reaching altitude and results in the initial increase in ventilation due to carotid body stimulation being increased slowly over this period to reach the final low level and, as we said, this then reduces the oxygen gradient between inspired and alveolar gas to about half that at sea level.

To disgress for a moment, in 1964 I had the opportunity with Dr S. Lahiri to study some differences between ourselves, acclimatised lowlanders, and Sherpas, lifelong residents at high altitude. We showed that for the same work rates, Sherpas had a lower ventilation. That is, they were physiologically more efficient. When we carried out these experiments breathing various oxygen and CO_2 mixtures, we were surprised to find their carbon dioxide response was similar to ours, but their hypoxic response was almost absent. This was confirmed by experiments on exercise when changing the inspired pO_2 made no difference to their ventilation, whereas it made a great difference to ours. This blunting of the ventilatory response to hypoxia has also been found in residents in the Andes but, oddly enough it is not found in animals born and bred at altitude.

Returning to our oxygen transport system (Figure 3), we see the next drop is due to the gas exchange loss of pressure. At altitude this is perhaps slightly reduced at rest, probably due to slightly greater blood flow through the lungs due to increased cardiac output.

However, there is a problem at exercise and John West on the Silver Hut expedition was the first to demonstrate this conclusively. He showed that the diffusing capacity at exercise was not significantly increased at altitude and that this normal diffusing capacity when operating at these low pressures was insufficient to allow enough oxygen across the lungs to maintain the oxygen level in the arterial blood during hard exercise. He showed that during maximal exercise at 19,000 ft the arterial oxygen saturation fell progressively as exercise continued, down to values as low as 45% saturation. This effect is shown in Figure 3 by the dotted line indicating the situation at maximum work.

The next step in the oxygen transport system is from the arterial to the mixed venous blood, and this mixed venous blood approximates to the tissue level. Again you will see a considerable reduction in this gradient at altitude. There are a number of causes contributing to this. First of all, the cardiac output at least at rest and on light exercise is increased. This means that the flow of blood through the tissues is increased and thus the amount of oxygen removed per unit volume of blood will be reduced. Another well known aspect of acclimatisation makes its contribution at this point, and this is the increase in red cells or in haemoglobin value that takes place at altitude. This change, which takes about six weeks to be complete, enables the blood to carry more oxygen per unit volume. At sea level haemoglobin allows 20 ml of oxygen to be carried per 100 ml of blood and, as blood is almost fully saturated, the actual content carried is 19.2 ml. At altitude the capacity is increased to 26 ml per 100 ml of blood because of the increase in the haemoglobin so that, although the blood is only 70% saturated with oxygen, the content is 18.2 ml per 100 ml. At slightly lower altitudes the arterial blood carries as much oxygen per 100 ml as at sea level. But probably the most important way in which this pressure gradient is reduced is due to the unique properties of haemoglobin and the way it combines with and gives up oxygen. As the pO_2 is reduced in arterial blood, oxygen comes off, but only a small amount comes off as the pressure is reduced to about $50 - 60$ mm Hg, and for each further drop in pO_2 much more oxygen is given off. At sea level, therefore, to obtain the necessary amount of oxygen in the tissues the pressure must drop from about 100 to 40 mm Hg whereas, at altitude, where the arterial pO_2 is down to the level where oxygen is being given off for a small pressure drop, a reduction from about 40 to 25 mm Hg is sufficient.

The result of all these adaptive changes is that the mixed venous level at altitude is only slightly lower than that at sea level at rest, although at heavy work rates the reduction is considerable. Beyond this point, in the cells themselves, it is very likely that adaptive mechanisms are taking place, but about these we know next to nothing.

Ill effects of hypoxia. The effects of hypoxia on the body that we have so far considered have been grouped under the heading of acclimatisation, that is changes that are considered beneficial to the body. There are many other effects of hypoxia. Indeed, since oxygen is a vital part of the living process, virtually every system of the body is potentially affected by hypoxia, though some are more resistant than others, and we need to consider briefly some of these other changes which do not appear to be particularly beneficial. The effect of hypoxia on the blood vessels of the lungs is to cause them mildly to constrict, thus increasing the pulmonary artery pressure. This is revealed by changes in the electrocardiogram which we also studied in the Silver Hut expedition. The main change is a shift to the right in the electrical axis of the heart. This is an effect seen in virtually all individuals on acclimatisation to altitude. We found in general that on increasing altitude from 15,000 to 25,000 feet there is a strong tendency for the axis to shift further and further to the right. This we think is due to the fact that the right ventricle is having to work harder against the increased resistance of the pulmonary circulation, due to hypoxic constriction of its vessels. This mechanism may be important in the causation of acute pulmonary oedema of high altitude, which we will be hearing about later. There are almost certainly changes also in the body water, both in amounts and in its distribution in the various compartments of the body, possibly through mechanisms of changes in endocrine function of the body, and Professor Williams has dealt with some of these already. These changes may also play a role in the causation of cerebral oedema and of acute mountain sickness. But at present the evidence on these water shifts is contradictory.

Altitude deterioration. It was pointed out in Figure 2 that the highest residence in the world was 17,000 feet and our experience of the Silver Hut expedition led us to believe that it was not possible to live indefinitely at altitudes much above this height. The reason for this is that, while the process of acclimatisation continues, other processes known collectively as altitude deterioration, cut in above this altitude and become more severe with each thousand feet ascended. The processes of altitude deterioration have not been studied at all. The condition, which is purely descriptive, is that of people who become fatigued, tire easily, lose weight despite adequate intake, and fail to recover from heavy exercise. No doubt, in many expeditions exposure, starvation and dehydration have all contributed to the general picture but, even when these are avoided, it seems that severe hypoxia alone can cause this condition of deterioration. The aspect of weight loss despite an adequate intake led us to examine the possibility that people severely hypoxic might have a degree of small bowel malabsorption. It was our impression that our stools at altitude tended to be more greasy and so we thought perhaps fat, at least, was not being absorbed properly. In 1972 I was able to examine a number of patients who were severely hypoxic due to either respiratory or cardiac conditions, and carried out a simple test of small bowel absorption, known as a xylose absorption test. This did show low and below normal values in these patients and, by and large, the patients who were most severely hypoxic had the lowest values. Perhaps more convincingly, in those patients in whom we were able to correct the hypoxia either by oxygen breathing or by cardiac surgery, we were able to show that there was an improvement in the xylose absorption test in every case. So far we have not had the opportunity to study this in climbers at really high altitude. In preliminary studies during a private expedition to the Everest base camp in 1971 we were able to show that up to 17,000 feet there was no impairment of xylose absorption, but only one night was spent at 17,000 feet.

The other aspect of deterioration which we are currently studying is that symptom of the failure to recover from exhausting exercise. The main fuel for muscles is glycogen. Swedish workers have shown that at the sort of level of exercise in which climbers are interested, that is fairly high physical exercise which exhausts one in a matter of a few hours, the level of muscle glycogen at the start of exercise seems to determine the length of time that exercise can continue. Further, they have shown that at the end of such exercise the glycogen is almost completely depleted from the working muscles. It is replaced when on a high carbohydrate diet in a couple of days and half the glycogen is replaced in about seven hours. We speculated that perhaps at high altitude this synthesis of muscle glycogen was greatly slowed, since it is an energy-using biochemical pathway and lack of oxygen might well mean a reduction in high energy phosphate bonds available for this process. We are currently carrying out experiments to test this and preliminary results seem to support this hypothesis.

Although we are now studying the deleterious effect of hypoxia, it does seem that all these effects are completely reversible and leave no lasting ill effects.

In fact, those climbers who have gone highest have had outstandingly successful careers afterwards. Those involved in these studies have, almost without exception, returned to the high mountains and I certainly hope to do so again!

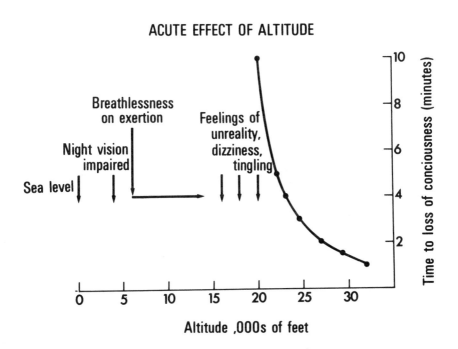

Figure 1. Effects of sudden exposure to increasing altitude.

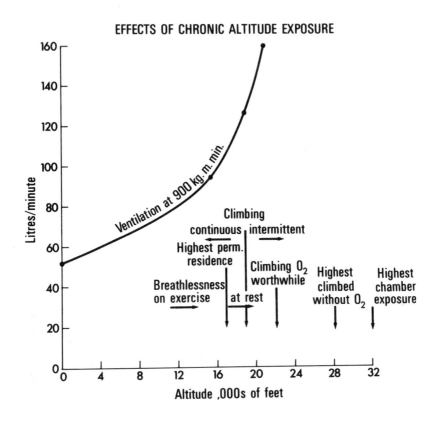

Figure 2. Effect of increasing altitude on acclimatised man.

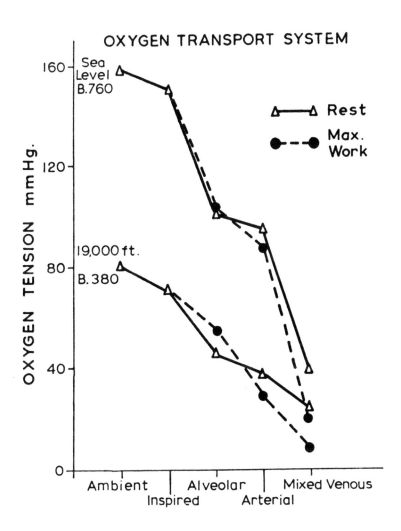

Figure 3. The oxygen transport system of man at sea level and acclimatised at 19,000 ft (Barometric pressure 380 mm Hg).

(from Pugh, 1964)

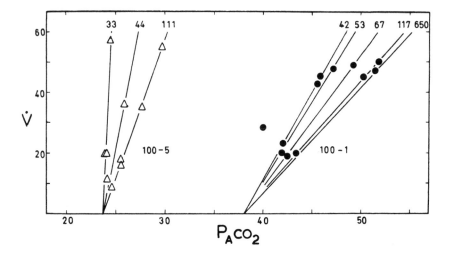

Figure 4. Ventilatory response of one subject at sea level (right hand "fan of lines") and at latitude, 19,000 ft (left hand "fan").

$\dot{V}$ = ventilation in litres/min, $pA_{co_2}2$ = alveolar CO_2 pressure. Points determined by breathing gas mixtures containing various proportions of CO_2 and O_2. The numbers at the ends of the lines indicate the pO_2 of that response line. (see text)

References

1 Milledge, J. S. Respiratory Regulation at 19,000 ft. In 'The Regulation of Human Respiration'. p 397–407. *Ed. Cunningham D.S.C. and Lloyd, B.B. Blackwell, Oxford, 1963.*

2 Milledge, J.S. (1963) Electrocardiographic changes at high altitude. *Brit. Heart J. 25,* 291–298.

3 Milledge, J.S. and S. Lahiri (1967). Respiratory control in lowlanders and sherpas highlanders at altitude. *Resp. Physiol. 2,* 310–322.

4 Milledge, J.S. (1972) Arterial oxygen desaturation and intestinal absorption of xylose. *Brit. Med. J., ii,* 557–8.

5 Pugh, L.G.C.E. (1962). Physiological and medical aspects of the Himalayan Scientific and Mountaineering Expedition 1960–61. *Brit. Med. J., ii,* 621–626.

6 Pugh, L.G.C.E. Man at high altitude. *Scientific Basis of Medicine Annual Reviews* 32–54, 1964.

7 "Life at high altitude". Ed. Weihe, W.H. *Proceedings of the Washington Meeting,* June 1966.

Discussion

Dr. Ballance. Can you tell us about unloading oxygen?

Dr. Milledge. At altitude there is less diphosphoglycerate. This shifts the oxygen dissociation curve to the left. The change of the dissociation curve is desperately small. There is no physiological significance. The change is of the order of 2–3 mm Hg.

Physiologists present discussed this point in detail but it was apparent that, for the mountaineer, the effect had no practical implications.

Dr. Edwards. I would like to draw attention to the studies of Reynafarje* (1962) which showed increased myoglobin and oxidative enzymes in muscle of high altitude residents in the Andes.

(*Reynafarje, Baltazar (1962) 'Myoglobin content and enzymatic activity of muscle and altitude adaption'. *J. Appl. Physiol. 17,* 301–305.)

Dr. Ward. Some Sherpas don't have high haemoglobin counts. Would you care to comment?

Dr. Milledge. Yes. It is useful to increase the haemoglobin for acclimatisation. But the amount you increase it to does not seem to be important. The price you pay for the increased haemoglobin is increased viscosity. This is not just a linear increase. It gets very steep above 20 G/100 ml. In South American it actually causes trouble.

Dr. Warren. Is'nt it dangerous, this viscosity?

Dr. Rennie. Agreed. I would bleed my climbers if they would agree to it.

Dr. Edwards. What happens in the heart muscle is also important.

Prof. Moore. It is said that above 170—180 beats a minute the heart loses efficiency. The advantage of speedy beating is therefore lost. The Sherpas were shown as going up to 200 and more. They must be able to fill the atrium at a very fast rate.

High Altitude Oedema—
Cerebral and Pulmonary

DRUMMOND RENNIE

I shall discuss two facets of Acute Mountain Sickness, cerebral œdema and pulmonary œdema, both of them killing diseases. They occur exclusively at high altitudes and being "high" as we now know, means being short of oxygen. The discovery of the disorder and the element almost coincided.

John Mayow, in 1674, showed that there was something in the atmosphere which an animal required for life and when the animal had used this something, it died.

Stephen Hales, in 1727, putting a candle, instead of an animal, inside the bell jar showed that the air supported combustion up to a certain point — using up that "something" that Mayow's animal had required. He showed that the animal used up one thirteenth part of the atmosphere before dying whereas the candle used up one eleventh before going out.

At the end of the 18th century, Antoine Lavoisier, chemist, and, incidentally, Comptroller-General of finances in France, isolated and discovered what that something was — oxygen. While his contemporary, the remarkable scientist and mountaineer Horace Benedict de Saussure, was publishing the results of his physiological, meteorological and geological studies, many of them made at high altitude on Mount Blanc — a mountain that was climbed very largely because of his interest, enthusiasm and money and of which he made the second ascent. De Saussure had plenty to say about the discomforts of mountain sickness.

Simultaneously, in this extraordinary age, the Montgolfier brothers had successfully launched the first balloon — a hot air machine which was succeeded by the hydrogen balloon of the French physicist, Charles, and the disastrously combined hot-air and hydrogen balloon of Madame Blanchard. The balloonists were soon experiencing the very acute and immediate effects of hypoxia, or lack of oxygen.

Ballooning reached its culminating point in 1875 with the astonishing scientific flight of Tissandier, Croce-Spinelli and Sivel, who reached a height of around 25,000 feet; when they reached the ground again, Tissandier was unconscious, the other two were dead — like Mayow's small animals.

Paul Bert, lawyer, physiologist, founder of Aerospace Medicine, politician, anti-cleric, woman's libber and finally Governor General of French Indo-China, published in 1878 "La Pression Barometrique", a book nearly 1200 pages long, half of it devoted to the history of high altitude physiology and the rest to his formidable researches. In this book there are numerous descriptions of Acute Mountain Sickness and equally many of the acute effects of hypoxia.

Meanwhile, Edward Whymper was one of the more determined enthusiasts leading climbers in ever increasing numbers into the mountains to enjoy the sport and ensure that there would be plenty of people around to get Acute Mountain Sickness.

What is Acute Mountain Sickness? I shall leave the description to Dr. T. H. Ravenhill, physician to a mining Company up in the Andes near the Chilean-Bolivian border. He wrote this in 1913, and I like it because his classification fits in with mine. He had an ideal opportunity, as he recognised, to see people who had been taken up effortlessly to high altitude in a short time (that is to around 16,000 feet in 42 hours from the coast), unaffected by exercise, fatigue, insufficient food and the normal trials of mountaineers. "It is a curious fact that the symptoms of puna (Acute Mountain Sickness) do not usually evince themselves at once. The majority of newcomers have expressed themselves as being quite well on first arrival. As a rule, towards the evening, the patient begins to feel rather slack and disinclined for exertion. He goes to bed, but has a restless and troubled night, and wakes up next morning with a severe frontal headache. There may be vomiting, frequently there is a sense of oppression in the chest, but there is rarely any respiratory distress or alteration in the normal rate of breathing so long as the patient is at rest. The patient may feel slightly giddy on rising from bed, and any attempt at exertion increased the headache, which is nearly always confined to the frontal region.

On examination, the face may be slightly cyanosed; the eyes look dull and heavy, with a tendency to water; the tongue is furred. The pulse is nearly always high, being generally in the neighbourhood of 100 or over. 150 was the highest in my cases. The temperature is normal or slightly under; not often is there any rise in temperature at first, though it may rise towards evening. There is at times reduplication of the pulmonary second sound. The patient feels cold and shivery.

The headache increases towards evening, so also does the pulse rate; all appetite is lost, and the patient wishes to be left alone -- to sleep if possible. Generally, during the second night he is able to do so, and as a rule wakes next morning feeling better; the pulse rate has probably dropped to about 90; the headache is only slight. As the day draws on, he probably feels worse again, the symptoms all tending to reappear on any exertion; if, however, he keeps to his bed, by the fourth day after arrival he is probably very much better, and at the end of a week is quite fit again. The most prominent feature in this type of puna is frontal headache and extreme lassitude."

He notes all the principal features of Acute Mountain Sickness: its occurrence after rapid ascent, even without exertion, to high altitudes; its delayed onset; its primarily cerebral symptoms; its short time course and its excellent prognosis. Its delayed onset in particular separated it from the acute effects of hypoxia described by the balloonists.

Ravenhill then goes on to note two very serious and even fatal divergences from the "normal" type of Acute Mountain Sickness, or puna, as it was called in the Andes, a "cardiac" form and a "nervous" form. He gives descriptions of three cases of the "cardiac" form of puna, one of whom was successfully evacuated to the coast, but the other two died. There is no doubt at all that these cases were really cases of pulmonary oedema. Ravenhill, interestingly enough, noted that this condition was not associated with weakness nor disease of the heart beforehand even though he thought that the altitude must affect the heart to cause heart failure.

I keep naming hypoxia as the primary cause, but I am very fully aware that there are numerous other factors at work in individual cases: exertion, fatigue, heat, sunlight, cold, dehydration and fear to name only a few.

I would like to follow Ravenhill's broad classification, modifying it in proposing that there are two main types of Acute Mountain Sickness, and that *both* are due to water being in the wrong place.

There is water in the brain which causes the symptoms of Acute Mountain Sickness, and, if very severe, this constitutes cerebral oedema. There is water in the lungs and if this is severe, it manifests itself as pulmonary oedema. I am going to explain what I understand by these statements, but first, does this matter? Yes. The two extreme manifestations of Acute Mountain Sickness *kill* people, and because these are people who go up into the mountains, they kill the young, the fit, the enthusiastic, the audacious and the physically hardworking, and they are killing them in ever-increasing numbers. In short, people taken suddenly to high altitude, spring internal fatal leaks.

I shall discuss water in the brain first — causing Acute Mountain Sickness if there is only a little and the signs of severe cerebral oedema if there is a lot — and then pulmonary oedema, which may be partly caused by cerebral oedema and which undoubtedly makes cerebral oedema very much worse.

Cerebral Oedema

What causes cerebral oedema? I have already mentioned that I think that this is due principally to water getting into the cells of the brain. What evidence is there for this? Looking into the old literature, it is very interesting that Forbes and his colleagues at Harvard back in 1924 (which is the year that Mallory and Irvine perished on Everest), discovered that if they made dogs or cats very short of oxygen by making them breathe carbon monoxide, and if this was done suddenly, the animals developed a considerable vasodilatation of the cerebral and retinal vessels.

If this was done more slowly, there was an increase in the brain volume due to water getting into the cells. This increase in brain volume could be cured by running high concentrations of a saline solution into the animal's blood stream. This solution would suck water out of the brain cells and shrink them by osmosis.

Obviously, this is a rather difficult phenomenon to investigate in man. The great Italian altitude physiologist, Angelo Mosso, working at the turn of the century in Turin and on Monte Rosa, had wondered whether the cause of Acute Mountain Sickness was dilatation of the blood vessels going to the brain. His clinical observations, which again fit in with Ravenhill's and mine, made him believe that all the signs and symptoms of Acute Mountain Sickness were fundamentally due to an upset of the nerve centers, placed at the base of the brain, which controlled all the vital functions such as the heart rate, breathing and so on. In Mosso's famous "Life of Man On the High Alps", he starts the chapter entitled "Circulation of the Blood in the Human Brain" with the memorable words: "It was my wish to find some man with a hole in his skull who would have been willing to come with me on the Monte Rosa Expedition, but I was not successful in my search. Some other physiologist will, I hope, be luckier."

Mosso was imagining what would happen if the pressure in the brain was raised. The skull is a rigid box: the brain has nowhere to go. The signs and symptoms of raised intra-cranial pressure depend on the speed of its onset and its severity, just as in the animals whom Forbes asphyxiated with carbon monoxide.

In fact, worse than having nowhere to go to, the brain tries to bulge out through rigid holes and past rigid projections. This not only fuddles the intellect, fogs the psyche and dulls the emotions, it can paralyse, render unconscious, stop the breathing and kill.

The theory then is that on exposure to high altitude water gets into the brain. At the same time there is dilatation of the blood vessels. In other words, both brain cells and blood vessels attempt to take up more space.

The skull, as Hansen and Evans have pointed out, is a box with holes covered by semi-elastic membranes. By Pascal's law, small volume changes cause large pressure changes. Large pressure changes cause everything from headache to slowing of the pulse to insomnia to death.

Why should water go into the cells at high altitude? This is arguable. It is probable that the cells aren't very good at keeping water out when they become hypoxic. It has also been suggested that the extra-cellular fluid, that is the fluid bathing the cells, loses its salts through the kidneys and therefore becomes very weak and dilute. The water is then sucked into the cells just by osmosis.

Mosso eventually got hold of two boys with holes in their skulls. In experiments with the first in a low-oxygen chamber, he seemed to show dilatation of the vessels, but he could not show it with the second. In fact, we now know that the cerebral blood flow increases about 30 or 40% at altitude and there is an associated dilatation of the cerebral vessels. These dilated vessels may compress the entire brain evenly or just cause local signs by pressing on particular parts of the brain, for example, that part in control of balance.

If the cerebral oedema becomes very severe, the cerebral blood flow just simply stops — so does the climber. At the same time, there may actually be blockage of some of the brain capillaries — the smallest blood vessels — and numerous little haemorrhages. In every case of cerebral oedema at high altitude brought to autopsy the bulging brain has been found to be covered with tiny haemorrhages as well as bigger ones within it. Big or small, these haemorrhages do the brain no good at all and they certainly indicate very severe, even catastrophic, cerebral upheaval, like gun shot in a computer.

If one assumes that the eye is window not merely to the soul, but also to the brain, then perhaps when we look into the eye and at blood vessels lying on the retina at the back, we are also being given a clue as to what is happening within the cerebral vessels locked within the bony skull.

In our group, Dr. Regina Frayser, has spent a great deal of time taking retinal photographs and measuring retinal blood flows on the plateau of Mount Logan in the Canadian Yukon. I have also continued this work on Dhaulagiri I, in the Himalayas.

In both situations, there was a 20% increase in diameter of arteries and veins in people taken to high altitude (17,500 feet on Logan or, at Base Camp on Dhaulagiri, 19,400 feet). This dilatation was associated with a big decrease in the amount of time taken for the blood to go through the eye and so a big increase in blood flow. Regina Frayser measured blood flow by injecting fluorescent dye into an arm vein and watching it go through the eyes.

The vessels, then, become fat and dilated and showed an increased flow. They also burst, forming mini-haemorrhages which occurred in about one third of people on Logan and in one third of the climbers on Dhaulagiri. This showed that they weren't related to the absolute height reached, nor to the level of exertion, both of which were very much higher on Dhaulagiri. This is a complicated matter, however, because the Dhaulagiri climbers had selected themselves out as being people who did well at very high altitudes. Perhaps an unselected group at these higher altitudes would have had a higher incidence of haemorrhages — but how do you get an 'unselected group' to 25,000 or 26,000 feet?

Why do these haemorrhages — retinal and cerebral — occur? Well, when you are straining, for example, on the pot, or lifting weights, or when doing a Valsalva manoeuvre or having a prolonged coughing fit, the pressure in your thorax goes up enormously. There are frightening physiological studies which show that just picking up weights by the arms will increase your blood pressure enormously. Think of this next time you carry a suitcase. You should definitely put it in a rucksack.

I coughed enough to go unconscious at 23,500 feet and broke two ribs in the process — or found I had done so when I woke up hanging from the fixed rope on my jumars. These intrathoracic pressures are, I believe, referred directly along fully dilated vessels to the already damaged and dilated capillary vessels in the eye and brain and in the brain the vicious cycle of haemorrhage, increased pressure and worsening cerebral oedema occurs. Of course, there may be clotting going on within the brain capillaries which increases the haemorrhagic tendency.

What are the symptoms of cerebral oedema or the nervous 'puna'? It is rare for it to be very severe, though, as I have said, mild cerebral oedema — the very mildest, probably accounts for acute mountain sickness. Well, you get very severe headache, dizziness, staggering, difficulty with respiration, the miserable Cheyne-Stokes respiration, bad dreams, hallucinations, double vision, paralysis, coma and death. It is as well to know that death can happen pretty rapidly.

Once at 15,200 feet on Dufourspitze of Monte Rose, a man I was climbing with became absolutely crazed and wanted to throw himself down the Macugnaga Face. We trussed him to a rock and while having lunch I meditated on the effects of a little cerebral oedema. Two or three years later, and more than 2,000 feet higher, I was able to meditate, fuzzily, on the effect of plenty of cerebral oedema — in the patient who was a pilot for the Canadian forces, as well as a cross-country running champion and who, 26 hours after being flown to 17,500 feet, was deeply unconscious with retinal haemorrhages and papilloedema — swelling of the optic nerve indicating cerebral oedema.

The only drug that has been consistently shown to be of prophylactic use in Acute Mountain Sickness is one that is known to have quite profound effects upon the brain. This is Diamox (Acetazolamide). It is known to raise the cerebral blood flow, but it reduces the formation of the fluid that bathes the brain, the cerebro-spinal fluid, and reduces the pressure of this fluid. It tends to increase breathing by making the cerebro-spinal fluid acid and it also acts as a mild diuretic, though this is probably its least important action in this connection. If taken before going up to high altitude and for a few days afterwards, it probably reduces the incidence of acute mountain sickness. It also ruins the taste of beer.

As I shall emphasize repeatedly in discussion of pulmonary oedema, (a much commoner serious manifestation of acute mountain sickness than serious cerebral oedema), I am very much against taking prophylactic drugs because the only true prophylactic is to go slowly and only go as high as *you* (not the others) feel fit to go. I cannot exaggerate the importance of prevention by simple common sense.

What is the treatment of cerebral oedema? The first and absolutely imperative thing is to get the person down to lower altitudes. Even quite a small decrease in altitude may save somebody's life. We recorded one man who drove his car up to 8,400 feet and then went on skis carrying a pack, was deeply unconscious at 10,500 feet, but rapidly recovered consciousness when brought down 2,000 feet to 8,400 feet. Whatever other procedures that you intend to do, for heaven's sake get the person down even if it means doing it at night and under bad conditions, because this will save the person's life. In this way, for example, Al Read's life was undoubtedly saved when he went unconscious on Daulagiri in 1969.

Give oxygen in the unlikely event that you have it to give, but *do not* delay getting the person down because you have got oxygen with you.

Climbers will go to great lengths to avoid being given injections of drugs by other climbers. However, in a nauseated, vomiting or unconscious man, pills may not go down — or stay down. Neurosurgeons will give steroid tablets or injections to decrease cerebral oedema and if you have got a doctor who has diagnosed this condition, then you should do the same: prednisone, dexamethasone or betamethasone. We would give 10mg of dexamethasone into a vein and then 6mg every 6 hours into the muscles. Steroids begin to work in six hours, however, and a maximal effect takes 24 hours. Before you go to high altitude, get a doctor to show you how, and where, to give intra-muscular injections, and with what steroid.

Osmotic diuretics (such as 20% mannitol or the hypertonic saline used by Forbes in his cats and dogs) will suck the person, and his brain, dry like a prune but they are difficult to give. Mannitol requires a blood infusion apparatus and bladder catheterization and is really not feasible on any but large expeditions. Injectable solutions tend to freeze and it is really awkward giving intravenous injections in very sick patients. More important, perhaps, is the simple care of the unconscious patient which includes cleaning his vomit out of his throat and catheterizing his bladder. This last is something I have had to do at high altitude, but it is not something a layman should be asked to do.

Practically, then, if you think someone has cerebral oedema, *get them down,* but as the condition is very awkward to manage and can be rapidly fatal, *prevent* it by going up the mountain in a leisurely manner.

Pulmonary Oedema

We now come to high altitude pulmonary oedema (which, because I live in the U.S.A., I call H.A.P.E., not H.A.P.O.). This is far commoner than the other severe manifestation of Acute Mountain Sickness, severe cerebral oedema. Pulmonary oedema is undoubtedly associated with hypoxia or lack of oxygen and it very rapidly makes this lack of oxygen worse, thus tending to precipitate cerebral oedema.

In the normal circulation, the heart pumps blue unoxygenated blood into the lungs where it is fully oxygenated, to a bright red colour. It returns to the left ventricle of the heart and this oxygenated, red blood, is then pumped around the body.

One of the lung's most important functions is to keep dry. Water constantly squeezes out of the tiniest pulmonary blood vessels, the capillaries, governed by hydrostatic and osmotic forces, and this water has to be drained away into the lymphatics, lest the alveoli — the smallest air sacs — flood.

In high altitude pulmonary oedema, the lung is full of water. As a result, blood goes into the lung normally blue but returns from the lung either not red enough or almost completely blue, that is, unoxygenated. Since the pulmonary oedema itself is associated with a lack of oxygen (in the atmosphere), this extra blueness of the blood makes the pulmonary oedema worse in a vicious cycle. There is no question that pulmonary oedema is associated with cerebral oedema and the worst cases of cerebral oedema have all got pulmonary oedema.

The lung itself consists of a sponge of alveoli or air sacs leading off small tubes connected to the trachea, called bronchioles. If the capillaries are separated from the alveoli by a thick wad of water, or the alveoli are flooded with water instead of air, or the capillaries are blocked, then the blood cannot be oxygenated.

What causes this pulmonary oedema? Well, Ravenhill, by naming this the "cardiac" form showed that he thought it was due to failure of the heart at high altitude, this failure being due to lack of oxygen. When the left ventricle is failing, it is unable to pump blood out into the body properly so pressures behind — that is, in the pulmonary veins — rise and the pressures in the smallest pulmonary vessels also rise, so water collects in the alveoli because of this pressure. Any doctor would, being educated and highly intelligent, think, like Ravenhill, that oedema of the lungs meant, not pulmonary failure, but heart failure — cardiac failure. Naturally, as Molière would have pointed out, he would be wrong: in pulmonary oedema occurring at high altitudes it was soon found out, after the report from Aspen, Colorado, of 1960, that the pressure in the left side of the heart and pulmonary veins was entirely normal and there was no evidence of left ventricular failure whatsoever. In other words, Ravenhill's 'cardiac' puna was pulmonary and not cardiac at all, which is precisely what any lay man would have guessed in the first place.

The cause is not heart failure, then, so what is it? I do not know: it is probable that several causes summate. The first possible cause is the increase in pressure in the pulmonary arteries which is known to occur in anyone going to altitude. This might make the capillaries leak, but only if the pressure is transmitted to the capillaries — but it is not. The pulmonary arteries themselves might leak with the increased pressure. The capillaries could leak because their walls are weakened by hypoxia (but this has never been shown to occur) or they might leak because some of them are overloaded because others are blocked by coagulated blood. This would cause a patchy pulmonary oedema which is, as you will see — exactly what you see on the chest x-ray. In several clinical situations, stimuli from an agonized brain may divert blood into the pulmonary circulation from the body or systemic circulation, thus, overloading the pulmonary circulation and causing seepage into the alveoli. There is good evidence that this sequence occurs in H.A.P.O. Finally, blockage of the capillaries could occur causing them to leak either because of little oedema vesicles or blebs sticking into the capillary lumens or because of clotting, itself set off by altitude exposure. This is known to occur and may be the most important cause of the whole process. Hypoxia narrows the pulmonary blood vessels, increases a great many of the blood factors involved in forming clots and decreases the blood factors that "lyse" or dissolve clots.

In my classification of high altitude troubles, I said that water went into the wrong places — brain and lungs — and this caused all the symptoms and signs of acute mountain sickness and of cerebral and pulmonary oedema. I have given evidence that the brain contains too much water. Do the lungs? Yes, they do. It is known that *all* people taken to high altitudes have more fluid in their chests and in high altitude pulmonary oedema this fluid is enormously increased.

Elaborate schemes have been devised to suggest why this should all happen: they are probably all completely wrong. It is known that there is, on exposure to lack of oxygen, an increase in hormones that retain sodium and, therefore, water and the central blood volume has a tendency, therefore, to increase, a tendency that is made greater by the fact that cold and a low carbon dioxide in the blood tends to constrict the veins and squeeze the blood into the chest. Prolonged exercise causes, according to Dr. Pugh, an increase in plasma volume and this will further increase the central blood volume. In addition, cerebral oedema will, through nervous impulses, cause a switch of blood to the pulmonary circulation, increasing the overloading of the pulmonary circulation.

Then the combination of high pulmonary artery pressure, pulmonary arterial leaking, capillary blockage and overload of other capillaries causes some of this extra fluid to end up in the alveoli.

Under what circumstances do climbers get pulmonary oedema? An important thing to remember is that there is an absolutely stupendous variation from one climber to the next. This variation is seen in all forms of Acute Mountain Sickness. It infuriated Whymper and Ravenhill was intrigued by it. First Ravenhill: "There is, in my experience, no type of man of whom one can say he will, or will not. suffer from puna. Most of the cases I have instanced were men to all appearances perfectly sound. Young, strong, and healthy men may be completely overcome; stout, plethoric individuals of the chronic bronchitic type may not even have a headache." On Chimborazo, at 16,664 feet, Whymper, the foremost mountaineer of his age, was having a bad attack of acute mountain sickness and was placed, with his companions, the two Carrels, completely out of action. Whymper wrote: "Strange to relate, Mr. Perring did not appear to be affected at all. Except for him, we should have faired badly. . ." He records that Mr. Perring kept the fire going, fed them and brought them drink and attended to their wants in general: his conduct was exemplary. Yet, at sea level, in the normal course of things "he was a rather debilitated man, and was distinctly less robust than ourselves. He could scarcely walk on a flat road without desiring to sit down, or traverse a hundred yards on a mountainside without being obliged to rest." One can summarize by saying that H.A.P.O. occurs in some individuals who go too high for themselves. Some may be stricken below 9,000 feet and others at 19,000 feet.

H.A.P.O. implies not merely that the altitude is too high for any one individual, but that it was reached too fast. Again there is tremendous variation. Charlie Houston records one person who had two attacks of pulmonary oedema at 8,500 feet, on the second occasion the patient had taken four days to get up to 8,500 feet, which is about as slow as it's possible to be. Mount Kenya, which is about 17,770 feet, is 2,000 feet lower than Kilimanjaro but has a far higher incidence of acute mountain sickness and pulmonary oedema than Kilimanjaro because Kenya can be climbed extremely rapidly and by people who are on package tours and Kilimanjaro forces one to spend several days trekking across country at quite high altitudes first. This, I believe, accounts for the fact that at the beginning of this century it was generally accepted that Acute Mountain Sickness occurred much more commonly in the Andes. Only in the Andes was there efficient transport – trains – capable of taking people rapidly from sea level to 16,000 feet altitude. One of the advantages of attacking Everest from the North is that one has to undertake a lengthy forced acclimatization march en route. The Chinese did this in rather large numbers though they missed out Everest and attacked the Indians instead. Very large numbers of Indians, thrashing their way up from the Ganges Valley, were overcome by Acute Mountain Sickness and pulmonary oedema. As one of the authors has repeatedly, even tediously, pointed out, Acute Mountain Sickness (with its children, pulmonary oedema and cerebral oedema) are very much diseases of civilization: affluence and impatience resulting in trains, cars, planes, helicopters and tight schedules. Everything conspires to push people too high, too fast.

What is the incidence of pulmonary oedema? As Ravenhill pointed out, it is certainly very much more common than severe cerebral oedema. Ravenhill thought that Acute Mountain Sickness was common and the cardiac type was fairly common. The trouble is that all the literature on the subject is anecdotal. There have been a flood of cases since that described by one of us in 1960, but it has been hard to get any good numerical study going.

In retrospect, many cases of 'pneumonia" (for example, Alfred Drexel, who died at 20,000 feet on Nanga Parbat in 1934, or Dr. Greene's case, the porter Ondi on Everest in 1933), were clearly cases of pulmonary oedema. At Chulec

Hospital, La Oroya in the Peruvian Andes at 12,300 feet, there are about 12 cases a year. Dr. Houston has reckoned that there are between 100 and 200 cases of pulmonary oedema world-wide each year, but I suspect that the real incidence is considerably greater than that. Singh found an incidence of 15.5% of pulmonary oedema in people with Acute Mountain Sickness, of whom he had over 1900 in the Indian army. Menon, however, found an incidence of 0.6%, and Singh noted that there were huge differences from one company of soldiers to the next. We are now well-embarked on an era of rationing of Mt. Rainier, and of packaged tours to Everest Base Camp and to Mt. Kenya: the incidence of pulmonary oedema is going up five or ten-fold.

What are the symptoms of H.A.P.O.? These are really important and climbers at high altitude should covertly watch for them in their companions. Given that people have a right to die if they wish, one should point out that the people we have seen with H.A.P.O. have been distinctly opposed to dying and that there have been several instances of rescuers dying from plane crashes and even pulmonary oedema. Moreover, one sick person at high altitude can put an entire party in peril.

Basically, the patient is much more severely breathless and weak than he should be at that altitude — in other words, than his companions are. He has usually got an irritating, hacking sort of cough and he may be spitting up bloody sputum. He may feel his chest bubbling, and it may be very easy for his companions to hear these bubbles. His breathing is irregular but usually very fast. He may become very rapidly moribund and very rapidly unconscious and very rapidly dead. From start to finish, the illness may take a few hours. It is essential to realize that this is a real emergency, requiring immediate action.

What you notice in your companion is that he is breathing rapidly, as if he had a hunger for air. His pulse is weak and rapid and he may have a bit of a temperature which makes you think of pneumonia (which he probably does not have). Often there is a great deal of pink or rusty sputum coming out and you can hear bubbles and gurgles going on in his chest. He is a deep blue colour. If it is very bad, he will lapse into coma when even the most unclinically orientated person will realize that something is wrong.

There are signs to be seen on the electro-cardiogram and chest x-ray, but these scarcely concern you, no matter how striking they are.

As with cerebral oedema and indeed with acute mountain sickness, the first thing (and I would say by *far* the most important thing) is to prevent it. Every effort should be made to go up the mountain slowly at first, the pace varying with the individual. Most people will be all right if they fly to 10,000 feet, spend two days there; climb a thousand feet a day to 14,000 feet and thereafter five hundred feet a day. Be intelligent about fixing climbing schedules. Carry high and sleep low, don't take gigantic loads huge distances, but divide them up, take longer and allocate more time and smaller loads. This advice I know to be very unpopular and, therefore, unacceptable. One three-month expedition to Logan came to us for advice on pulmonary oedema. We gave it. The very next day they flew to 9,000 feet, climbed for a whole night and a day to 12,000 feet and at 14,000 feet their youngest member almost died from pulmonary oedema.

I am absolutely against taking pills to prevent these diseases. They are marginally effective and are no substitute for intelligent planning; moreover, they have toxic effects. Dr. Raymond Greene published a paper in the 1930's showing the benefits of ammonium chloride in hypoxia – what an iron man.

Recognition. Always be suspicious of H.A.P.O. when climbing at highish altitudes, and that means anything over ten thousand feet, and just keep your eye on your companion. If a man has had pulmonary oedema before, he will, in my experience, be far more likely to have it again than the next man. It is said by some people that people who dwell at high altitude and who go down to low levels for a few weeks are twice as likely as the average person to get H.A.P.O. on "re-entry", but this is a very complicated statistic. Hultgren recorded that one person was admitted to Chulec Hospital on no less than ten separate occasions with pulmonary oedema after visits to the coast – a slow learner.

Treatment. As with cerebral oedema, *descend, give oxygen* and *rest* (but this time rest sitting up). By far the most important therapies are immediate descent (even a thousand feet may help) and rest. If you give oxygen, use a good, tight-fitting mask and aim at 6 to 8 litres per minute. This, of course, may be impossibly prodigal – you may not be able to afford more than 2 litres per minute.

What happens if you treat with oxygen? These treatments, particularly rest and descent, decrease the heart rate, the respiration rate and the temperature. We urge you not to rely on oxygen alone but to evacuate the patient to lower altitudes at all costs.

It is logical to give fluids because there is an extracellular dehydration with fluid moving into the cells and because water is lost with breathing and sweating and vomiting, but it is also logical to give diuretics to clear the lungs, which a powerful diuretic like "Lasix" (frusemide on this side of the Atlantic and furosemide on the other) is remarkably effective in doing. "Lasix" will also reverse the urine suppression (or oliguria) seen in patients with H.A.P.O., and with a brisk increase in urine output, drying out of the lungs is usually rapid. We strongly advise "Lasix" (40 to 120mg, by mouth) in the treatment (but *not* the prevention) of H.A.P.O.

In H.A.P.O., give fluids only if you know your diuretics are working well first – in other words, if the patient is passing lots of urine.

There are lots of very clever treatments that one can do in a hospital, such as Intermittent Positive Pressure Respiration and Positive End Expiratory Pressure. First of all, you cannot do the first (I.P.P.R.) on any mountain, and I am speaking to mountaineers, and P.E.E.P., which should open up the air passages all the way to the alveoli, is rather like grunt breathing and that has been responsible for at least three ruptured lungs with pneumothoraces on relatively low mountains, so we wouldn't advise it. No one, on a mountain, is set up for naso-tracheal suction and for acid-base regulation. We wouldn't give digitalis since the heart is fine, and by the same token, we would not use tourniquets to cut off venous return to the heart. Whether aminophylline is useful is arguable, but if you can persuade the climber to sit on an aminophylline suppository, you might open up his airways a little. So is the use of morphine, which we would definitely advocate in H.A.P.O. as it decreases anxiety and causes the peripheral veins to dilate, helping to shift blood away from the lungs. Its effects have, on several occasions, been dramatic.

The lungs will clear rapidly if you have brought the patient down to lower altitudes and if you are sitting him up and keeping him quiet. He may then be able to go climbing again. It takes longer for the electrocardiogram to become normal. An interesting thing is that people who have had pulmonary oedema on later testing have distinct differences in the way that they breathe and lower their blood carbon dioxide level at high altitude. They have a decreased oxygenation in the lungs and they have an increased pulmonary artery pressure. These results might mean that they are H.A.P.O.-susceptible people and may not indicate any after-effects of H.A.P.O., but a lot of people have been to high altitude after attacks of pulmonary oedema and not had an attack again.

I have talked about going high and, therefore, of going hypoxic, I have proposed that one of the body's responses to this is to shift water, either into cells (for example, into the brain, causing acute mountain sickness or, rarely, cerebral oedema) or into the alveoli of the lungs — which is pulmonary oedema. I have emphasized that the treatment is descent, rest and oxygen, but that treatment is difficult, hazardous and chancy whereas prevention, by leisurely ascent, is too simple and too obvious that no one will ever accept it in this impatient world.

Discussion

Dr. Houston. Drummond Rennie is the guiding light of most of our work at Logan. I have some observations.
1) Cerebral Oedema and Pulmonary Oedema do not necessarily occur in the same patient. We have had a number of unconscious cerebral oedema patients with clear lungs.
2) The time scale is confusing. Acute Mountain Sickness can occur within a few hours of arrival at high altitude. I have never had an oedema case within less than twelve hours of arrival at altitude. Consider the phenomenon in Colorado. As the convenient ski-resorts become crowded we have built 9,000 — 9,500 ft

base lodge ski resorts. I was shown a few cases at one of them of people who were based at 9,500 feet going to ski at 11,000 – 12,000 feet.

For instance: A healthy eleven year old boy arrived on the 2nd July. He skied the same day. On the third day he sprained his ankle and rested. At 8.15 pm on the third day he was dead on arrival at hospital. The X-ray was loaded with pulmonary oedema.

There must have been two other unequivocal cases of pulmonary oedema at that altitude. Stress, exertion, and rapid ascent will provide clinical material from lower altitudes than previously.

(3) The proposition that the human brain turns to peanut butter at high altitude is completely rebuffed by a number of people in this room. There is a feeling in the U.S.A. that no expedition should go above twenty thousand feet without oxygen.

Dr. Robertson. The solution that has been suggested is to bring the patient towards sea level. Why cannot sea level be brought towards the patient? It is possible to make a bag weighing two pounds and pressurize the man.

A speaker. There is no need ever for a bag. You could just apply the pressure to the lungs. In aviation medicine we have an automatic device to pressurize the patient at the time an incident occurs.

Hypoxia and the Heart

FREDERIC S. JACKSON

One of the earliest observations on the heart at high altitude was made by de Saussure in 1787 during the third ascent of Mont Blanc when he compared the rapid resting pulse rate on the summit with the slower rate after returning to Chamonix.

	Summit of Mont Blanc (15,782 ft.)	Resting at Chamonix (3,404 ft.)
Balmat (guide)	98	49
Prof. de Saussure	100	60
A servant	112	72

Table 1. The increase in pulse rate per minute with increasing altitude.

Interest in the effects of height on the heart has continued since that date, but because of the great difficulty in obtaining scientifically acceptable information much of what was said and written in earlier days borders on myth or fiction.

There are three main sources of knowledge about the effects of hypoxia on the heart, namely:

1. Studies made in decompression chambers.

2. Physiological measurements made in laboratories situated at high altitude notably in the Andes, in North America and in the Alps; the work of Barcroft in Peru in 1911 was among the earliest.

99

3. Observations made by scientists and doctors on mountaineering expeditions especially to the Himalaya.

The results obtained from these sources are not strictly comparable, because, in a decompression chamber the ascent is "passive", i.e. effortless, and usually of short duration — Houston's "Operation Everest" (1955) was a notable exception — whereas mountaineers undergo sustained physical exertion combined with a slower but prolonged exposure to hypoxia. Moreover in describing the effects of hypoxia on the heart we have to consider not only the *immediate* responses, but the *medium-term* effects — i.e. the changes which occur during acclimatisation, and the *long-term adaptations* which are seen in those born at high altitude or resident there for some years.

The most obvious effect of hypoxia is seen on the *heart rate*. During "passive ascent" and still more so during climbing to a high altitude the heart rate increases as the oxygen tension falls, as de Saussure noted. The increase in rate is roughly proportional to the height.

The rise in heart rate coincides with an *increase in cardiac output* of which it is the main determinant, a higher output being required to maintain tissue oxygenation when the oxygen content of the blood is diminished as a result of lowered atmospheric oxygen tension.

Very rapid heart rates, over 200 per minute, may be reached during exertion and sustained for considerable periods. Fig. 1 shows the ECG recorded on magnetic tape of a 25 year old man in good training while climbing between 17,000 and 19,000 ft. in the Sierra Nevada de Santa Marta.*

Changes in rhythm are surprisingly uncommon, apart from ventricular extrasystoles, of which one is shown in Fig. 1. Atrial ectopic beats or ectopic rhythms also occur. The only instance of atrial fibrillation related to hypoxia that I know of was in a medical student who swam a length of a bath underwater, though doubtlessly it must have occurred during mountaineering at some time or other.

Stroke volume changes less than the heart rate in response to hypoxia while at rest, but appears to exceed sea-level values at maximum work loads (Vogel et al 1967).

After the first week or so at high altitude the heart rate falls as other processes of acclimatisation occur such as the rise in the haemoglobin concentration and the probable shift of the haemoglobin-oxygen dissociation curve to the right (Astrup et al., 1968). The cardiac output too returns to normal by about the third week. In fully acclimatised men who had been several months at 19,000 ft Pugh (1962) found normal resting cardiac outputs but reduced maximum outputs at maximum work load.

The *blood pressure* normally alters very little with changes in altitude and appears to depend on other factors than hypoxia; it has been seen to rise slightly or to fall a little. The *mean* arterial pressure may rise when the heart rate

* The lightweight recorder was lent by the Oxford Instrument Company Ltd., Oxford.

increases without any rise in systolic pressure. The blood pressure in people living permanently at high altitudes is not often raised. In two surveys of Himalayan populations resident at over 12,000 ft. no cases of severe hypertension were discovered, and only a small percentage had moderately elevated levels. There is no evidence however why altitude *per se* should protect against the development of hypertension.

Hypoxia induces dilatation of peripheral vessels with a lowering of vascular resistance and permits an increase in cardiac output without a rise in systemic blood pressure. In particular the coronary arteries have been shown experimentally to dilate during hypoxia. Coronary flow is increased and improves myocardial perfusion thereby helping the heart to meet the higher work load thrust upon it. Against this however must be set the effect of shortened total diastolic time at faster heart rates in reducing the period during which coronary flow can occur; this can be expressed as a reduction in the ratio between the diastolic and systolic pressure-time indices.

One of the most interesting effects of hypoxia is reflex *constriction of the smaller pulmonary arteries* which leads to a rise in pulmonary arterial pressure. This effect was described by von Euler and Liljestrand in Sweden in 1946. It is found in animals as well as man, cattle being particularly susceptible, but varies considerably from individual to individual, and newcomers appear to be more susceptible than acclimatised residents. The reasons for this and the mechanism are imperfectly understood. It has been suggested that it is an attempt to redistribute the flow of blood through the lungs to the less well perfused upper lobes. Others have postulated an atavistic persistence of the pulmonary vaso-constriction which before birth prevents the blood from shunting purposelessly through the unventilated lungs (Dawes, 1968). Sustained pulmonary vaso-constriction after birth may account for the increased frequency of patent ductus arteriosus observed in the Andes and of primary pulmonary hypertension reported from Leadville (10,200 ft), Colorado.

The increase in pulmonary arterial pressure is thought to be mainly responsible for the very marked *rightward shift* of the electrical axis of the heart which is consistently seen in *electrocardiograms* taken at high altitude (Fig. 2). The predominantly upward deflection of the QRS complex in lead I at sea-level becomes mainly downwards at heights around 20,000 ft representing a shift in the mean frontal QRS axis of as much as $+50^\circ$. This is much greater than the rightward shift which can be produced by deep inspiration alone. Coupled with this change is a tendency of the T wave in lead V_1 to become inverted and sometimes for the *r* wave or the secondary *r* wave (r') in V_1 to become more prominent. These changes are thought to be due to overloading of the right ventricle in maintaining an increased output against an increased pulmonary vascular resistance. They also occurred in the cardiograms of Sherpa residents at high altitude taken to a greater height. They revert towards normal when the subject returns to sea-level.

After prolonged residence at high altitude, and in people born there, anatomical changes take place in the pulmonary vasculature and the right ventricle hypertrophies, but there is a very wide individual variation. In a yak's heart the muscle of the right ventricle was nearly as thick as that of the left. Post mortem examination of human hearts has shown increased right ventricular wall thickness (Recavarren and Arias-Stella, 1964).

However in two Himalayan population surveys at about 12,000 feet (Jackson, Turner and Ward, 1967; Jackson, 1968) there was a surprising lack of clinical or electrocardiographic evidence of pulmonary hypertension or of right ventricular hypertrophy though no direct measurements of pulmonary arterial pressure were made. The average of the mean frontal QRS axis of 117 adults in Sola Khumbu and Lunana differed by less than 10° from the average of 74 healthy Edinburgh adults. In the Andes however, the average axis of 200 adults at 15,000 feet and at sea-level differed by 70° (Peñaloza et al., 1961). A possible explanation is that the Tibetans have lived at these heights for so many thousands of years that they have outbred the reactivity of the pulmonary arteries to hypoxia, and that the Andeans may in genetic time be relative newcomers to the environment.

ST segment and T wave changes in leads over the left ventricle have been observed many times in mountaineers. One is tempted to ascribe such T wave inversion to myocardial ischaemia, possibly subendocardial, but there were no symptoms of angina. The explanation is uncertain. Recent work has shown that when the DPTI/SPTI ratio is reduced, as with a very fast heart rate, perfusion of the subendocardial muscle becomes selectively impaired (Brazier, Cooper and Buckberg, 1974).

Fig. 2 summarises the electrocardiographic changes observed at high altitude with some suggested mechanisms. Perhaps the most surprising fact of all, as Milledge (1963) said, is that the cardiograms of men who have climbed as high as 24,400 feet showed such little evidence of the severe physiological stress they were under.

The heart size. Earlier Everest climbers believed that the heart dilated under the severe stress of climbing at extreme heights. So far there has been no direct means of testing this because x-rays could not be taken, but other evidence suggests that this is not so. The apical impulse of the hyperdynamic heart is felt further to the left of the chest and conveys an erroneous impression of enlargement. Moreover x-rays of a climber taken before an expedition and immediately after returning rapidly to Katmandu from 20,000 feet suggest a slight *decrease* rather than an increase in heart size (Jackson and Davies, 1960), and one member of the 1962 Makalu expedition x-rayed within a few days of being at 24,000 feet showed no overall cardiac enlargement though the right ventricle and pulmonary artery were unduly prominent.

It may be asked what are the effects of hypoxia on a diseased heart and has it any long term adverse effects? Clearly a person with haemodynamic impairment will perform less well under the strain of hypoxia. This is particularly true of diseases where the pulmonary pressures are elevated, notable in mitral stenosis or with left ventricular damage. With aortic stenosis hypoxic stress is likely to be well tolerated up to a point but maximum load is probably diminished, and common sense would suggest that it is unwise to attempt this limit. With myocardial ischaemia from coronary disease symptoms usually limit performance automatically. There is no evidence that the hypoxic stress of climbing very high does permanent damage to the heart, and the healthy longevity of early Everest climbers bears witness to this. Some cardiologists think that repeated exposure to hypoxia with exertion stimulates the development of anastomotic blood vessels in the myocardium and in that sense has a positive protective action, but it is doubtful whether this has been substantiated.

There is still very much that is not known about the effects of hypoxia on the heart. Catheter studies at extreme heights, x-rays, continuously recorded electrocardiograms and perhaps echocardiographic records are needed. Using aircraft to transport generators to high locations, and with lightweight transisterised apparatus, float-catheters, telemetry and the like, exciting new physiological discoveries are likely to be made, but inevitably the cost will be considerable.

References

Astrup, P., Rørth, M., Mellemgaard, K., Lundgren, C. and Mulhausen, R.O. (1968). Changes of oxygen affinity of blood at low and high pressures. *Lancet, ii,* 732.

Dawes, G.S. (1968). Foetal and Neonatal Physiology, *Year Book Publishers Inc., Chicago.*

von Euler, U.S., and Liljestrand, G. (1946). *Acta Physiol. Scand. 12,* 301.

Houston, C.S. (1955). Some observations on acclimatization to high altitude. *New Eng. J. Med. 253,* 964.

Jackson, F. and Davies, H. (1960). The electrocardiogram of the mountaineer at high altitude. *Brit. Heart J. 22,* 671.

Jackson, F. (1968). The heart at high altitude (Editorial article). *Brit. Heart J. 30,* 291.

Jackson, F., Turner, R.W.D., and Ward, M.P. (1967). Himalayan Scientific Expedition to North Bhutan, 1965. Report to the International Biological Programme, *The Royal Society, London.*

Milledge, J.S. (1963). Electrocardiographic changes at high altitude. *Brit. Heart J. 25,* 291.

Peñaloza, D., Gamboa, R., Marticorena, E., Echevarría, M., Dyer, J. and Gutiezzez, E. (1960). The influence of high altitudes on the electrical activity of the heart. *Amer. Heart J. 61*, 101.

Pugh, L.G.C.E. (1962). Physiological and medical aspects of the Himalayan Scientific and Mountaineering Expedition 1960–61. *Brit. med. J. ii*, 621

Recavarren, S., and Arias-Stella, J. (1964). Right ventricular hypertrophy in people born and living at high altitudes. *Brit. Heart J. 26*, 806.

Vogel, J.A., Hausen, J.E., and Harris, C.W. (1967). Cardiovascular responses in man during exhaustive work at sea-level and high altitude. *J. app. Physiol. 23*, 531.

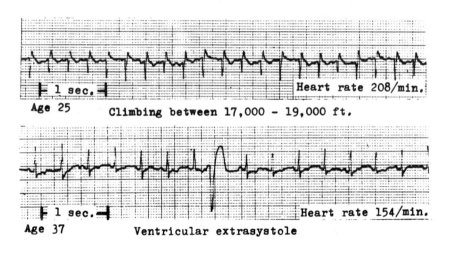

Figure 1. Electrocardiograms recorded on magnetic tape during climbing. Upper trace shows sinus tachycardia, 208 per min. Lower trace sinus tachycardia with a ventricular ectopic beat.

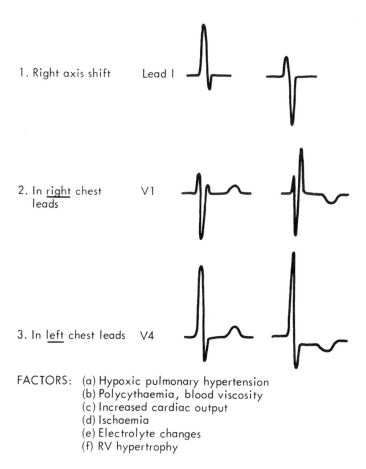

1. Right axis shift   Lead I

2. In <u>right</u> chest leads   V1

3. In <u>left</u> chest leads   V4

FACTORS: (a) Hypoxic pulmonary hypertension
             (b) Polycythaemia, blood viscosity
             (c) Increased cardiac output
             (d) Ischaemia
             (e) Electrolyte changes
             (f) RV hypertrophy

Figure 2. Principal changes in the electrocardiogram at high altitude. The traces on the left are taken from subjects at sea level, those on the right from the same subjects at altitude.

Discussion

Dr. Pawan. Is there any significant difference in the incidence of coronary heart disease between the lower Himalayan Populations and those at high altitudes?

Dr. Jackson. The numbers are small and it is difficult to conclude with certainty. We thought there was no angina. Skeletal pain is common anyway.

Mr. Ward. I thought cholesterol levels were low. Nothing significant. They have a mainly vegetable diet.

Prof. Moore. Is there an advantage in starting off with a stronger heart?

Dr. Edwards. There may be. There is in racehorses.

Prof. Moore. Pre-mountaineering exercises might help.

Anon. Irvine was a rowing man. So too was Tom Brocklebank.

Dr. F. Jackson. The longevity of Alpine Club Members has been studied and it is found that they live longer than average.

Physiology of Fitness and Fatigue

R. H. T. EDWARDS

'Fitness' has to do with the capability of mind and body to perform successfully a chosen task. Inability to perform the task to the expected standard is described as 'fatigue'. For the mountaineer the psychological aspects of fitness are based on the confidence that he possesses the necessary skill, strength, endurance and experience to complete his chosen climb. In physiological terms it means that the combined capacity of lungs, heart and circulation must be sufficient to supply the necessary oxygen to working muscles, that the metabolic fuels for muscular activity should be readily available and that the contractile machinery of the muscle is working normally. Fatigue will result if energy supply is insufficient but failure of the nervous system to drive the muscles is likely to be important in many circumstances, due to the compounding psychological effects of external influences (heat, cold, discomfort, etc.).

In mountaineering, muscles are used to support the body against gravity. The three most important uses are for climbing up, climbing down and for 'hanging' on. In physiological terms these describe three quite different forms of muscular contraction. When climbing up the muscle shortens as it contracts. This is known as 'positive' work. When climbing down, the muscle lengthens during contraction and this activity is known as 'negative' work. Both these forms of muscular contraction, if repeated frequently, constitute types of 'dynamic' exercise. When 'hanging on' the muscle length is unchanged during contraction and the activity is known as 'static' work (Isometric exercise). Positive work requires about six times as much energy expenditure as negative work. In isometric exercise no external work is performed, however, energy is required for sustaining the contraction and the rate of expenditure is directly dependent on the force of contraction.

Oxidative processes supply the energy for dynamic exercise, the fuels being muscle glycogen (the form carbohydrate is stored in animals) and blood-borne glucose and fatty acids. The capacity for oxygen transport, the 'maximal oxygen intake', is the best guide to fitness for long-continued dynamic exercise. Marathon runners and cross country skiers have the highest maximal oxygen

107

intake of all athletes when this is expressed in relation to body weight (over 70 ml $O_2.kg^{-1}min^{-1}$). Members of the 1953 Mount Everest expedition had a value which averaged 50 ml.$kg^{-1}min^{-1}$ (Pugh, 1958). It would, however, seem to be an advantage in climbing to have as high a 'power to weight' ratio as possible.

Dynamic exercise may be continued for several hours without fatigue providing the work rate does not demand an oxygen intake much greater than half the maximum oxygen intake. (However, marathon runners have an exceptional ability to work for long periods near their maximum oxygen intake). Mountaineers usually learn the right rate of climbing by experience (Pugh, 1958), but psycho-physical tests can also be used to measure the perception of exertion (Edwards, Melcher, Hesser, Wigertz & Ekelund, 1972). An easily accessible guide is the pulse rate which should not exceed 130/min if the work rate is to be sustained for several hours. At very high altitude the mountaineer may have little choice but to work near to his maximum oxygen intake and to adopt an intermittent exercise pattern (Pugh, 1958), even though this form of exercise appears to be more costly in physiological terms than working continuously at the same average work rate (Edwards, Ekelund, Harris, Hesser, Hultman, Melcher & Wigertz, 1973).

The endurance time in dynamic exercise, determined by the muscle glycogen concentration, can be extended by preserving a high muscle glycogen level both by increasing the resting muscle glycogen level by a regime of exercise and carbohydrate diet, and by feeding glucose during exercise. (For a review of these and other aspects of exercise physiology, see Åstrand & Rodahl, 1970.)

Since fatigue will occur sooner if there is discomfort, it is worth pointing out that negative work is more liable to cause muscle soreness than positive work (Asmussen, 1956) and is well known to carry a greater risk of musculo-skeletal injury. Running down hill can be hazardous.

In isometric exercise the principal energy supplies have to be provided from sources in the muscle since the circulation is arrested at contraction forces exceeding 20% of a maximum voluntary contraction. The time such a contraction can be sustained is short; a few seconds for a truly maximal effort since the force falls at about 1% of the initial force per second. A force of half maximum can be held for about 60 seconds and only with contractions less than 20% maximum can the force be sustained for more than 10 minutes. This type of activity makes very great demands on the local energy stores in muscle (see Edwards, 1975) however, fatigue is more likely to be due to failure of neural drive of the muscle than to failure of the contractile machinery or insufficient energy supply. The energy cost of maintaining a contraction is less in cold than in warm muscle (Edwards, Harris, Hultman, Kaijser, Koh & Nordesjö, 1972) but this effect is complicated by the fact that neural drive of the muscle begins to fail if cooling is severe. Cold muscles relax more slowly than normal and there is also marked (2–3 times) slowing of relaxation as the muscle becomes fatigued. Slowing of relaxation would reduce the maximum rate of working by the muscle and make skilled movements more difficult thus compounding the effects of fatigue. The force of a maximum voluntary isometric contraction depends on the cross-sectional area of the muscle. This depends to an important extent on the amount of activity the muscle is habitually given. Disuse leads to atrophy and loss of function in muscle as in other organs.

It is especially important for British mountaineers who may be in a position to undertake great alpine climbs only once a year to remember that disuse leads to atrophy and loss of function, and to check that their muscle strength and capacity for prolonged dynamic exercise is adequate before they begin the ascent. It is not feasible to do formal tests of exercise capacity and muscle strength but a number of simple performance tests can easily be devised to test personal 'fitness'. In an account of ice climbing, W.H. Murray (1961) wrote "The prime secret of high performance is confidence – born not only of familiarity with rock and ice, but also of physical fitness – confidence that every muscle will take the strains that come on it . . . I myself, being light and lean find that when able to run a mile and to do thirty press-ups, I am then in good enough training for severe ice. When I cannot do these things, I am not able to cope".

There are sound physiological reasons why training of mind and body are important in mountaineering. 'Fitness' implies the possession of sufficient reserves of functional capacity to allow long endurance and preservation of the necessary strengths and skills to deal with emergencies. During the climb it is worth the mountaineer making a conscious effort to monitor exertion and signs of fatigue in himself and other members of his party and to allow for fatigue when setting the rate of working. Carbohydrate must be taken by mouth to preserve muscle glycogen levels thereby extending endurance. Adverse environmental conditions (heat, cold, wind, wet, altitude and difficult terrain) accelerate the onset of fatigue in ways which are explicable in physiological terms. 'Fitness' and 'fatigue' are opposite sides of the same coin, as much for the mountaineer as for athletes in general. There is one important difference however; the mountaineer's life, or that of his companions may be in the balance if the standard of fitness does not match the standard of the climb.

References

Asmussen, E. Observations on experimental muscle soreness. *Acta Rheum. Scand.* 2, 109–116, 1956.

Åstrand, P. O. & Rodahl, K. A Textbook of Work Physiology. New York, *McGraw-Hill, 1970.*

Edwards, R.H.T., Melcher, A., Hesser, C.M., Wigertz, O. & Ekelund, L.-G. Physiological correlates of perceived exertion in continuous and intermittent exercise with the same average power output. *Europ. J. clin. Invest. 2,* 108–114, 1972.

Edwards, R.H.T., Harris, R.C., Hultman, E., Kaijser, L., Koh, D. & Nordesjö, L.-O. Effect of temperature on muscle energy metabolism and endurance during successive isometric contractions, sustained to fatigue of the quadriceps muscle in man. *J. Physiol. 220*, 335–352, 1972.

Edwards, R.H.T., Ekelund, L.-G., Harris, R.C., Hesser, C.M., Hultman, E., Melcher, A. & Wigertz, O. Cardiorespiratory and metabolic costs of continuous and intermittent exercise in man. *J. Physiol. 234*, 481–497, 1973.

Edwards, R.H.T. "Muscle Fatigue". *Postgrad. med. J. (In Press)*.

Murray, W.H. "Axe and crampon." *Mountaincraft No. 51* (April–June), 1961.

Pugh, L.G.C.E. "Muscular exercise on Mount Everest." *J. Physiol. 141*, 233–261, 1958.

Discussion

Dr. Steele. We found that the Baltoro porters would walk 50 to 100 yards and then stop for ten seconds. This is unlike the teachings of Winthrop Young. It seemed to them a better thing to do. (It *was*). The maximum oxygen intake becomes less and less as height is gained. So you have got to go slower and slower. It is inefficient because you are using more effort just to keep your balance. So we walk briskly, then stop; walk briskly, and stop again.

Sir Jack Longland. Fifty minutes march and ten minutes halt was the rule in the Army.

Dr. Nicol. It is most important if people are to stop that they do so in a heat-conserving position. It is particularly true in the Cairngorms that you are not rendered safe merely by stopping in a bivouac area.

Prof. Williams. Children and young people are particularly at risk. They are on a knife edge.

Dr. Edwards. It is important to have a high muscle glycogen before a hard rock climb because intense demands are made upon the muscles for a short time.

Fitness and the Relation of Terrain and Weather to Fatigue and Accidental Hypothermia in Hill Walkers

J. R. BROTHERHOOD

Fitness and fatigue

A wide range of individual ability may often be observed amongst people enjoying outdoor pursuits that involve long periods of physical exercise. In hill walking, even on the gentlest tourist routes, some cover the ground much more rapidly than others. Many must also have had the experience of being 'out of their league': trying to keep up with others faster than themselves; a circumstance at the best demoralising, but sometimes frightening and even dangerous. Although there may be many reasons for these individual disparities 'moral fibre' cannot entirely account for them and much can be explained and appreciated physiologically.

The stresses of physical activities such as mountaineering largely arise from the energy demands made upon the participant. These demands upon the climber are imposed by a number of factors, his speed of progression, clothing and load, the terrain he is traversing and the weather. Energy is generally required only for the physical work involved but under certain circumstances may also be required to maintain body heat.

Fitness in this context may best be defined as the individual's present ability to cope with the demands of his pursuit, and is therefore not necessarily a state that has been achieved by training.

In mountaineering and hill walking, this ability then has two main components, the individual's ability to perform physical work and his endurance. Fatigue is the state that occurs during prolonged exercise when the individual can no longer sustain his initial energy production and may regain it for brief periods only with considerable effort.

Energy for muscular work or heat production is obtained in the body by the metabolism of fats and glucose with oxygen. It is found that the individual's capacity to perform muscular work is limited by the maximum rate at which his lungs and circulation can supply oxygen from the air to his muscles. This is known as the maximum oxygen uptake and coincides with the maximum power production that can be supported for more than a minute or so. The range of individual working capacities in the population is at least two-fold. It appears to be genetically endowed and can be improved only to a moderate degree — say 10–15% — by training. For the average person it reaches its peak in the early twenties and declines after 25–30 years of age. Women have capacities some 30% lower than men.

The physiological strain arising from physical activity and endurance, are both determined not so much by the actual demands of the activity but by the proportion of the individual's capacity that it involves. So that the same activity may be more stressful to one person, and require more effort, than to another with a higher maximum oxygen uptake.

Maximal power outputs are extremely stressful and can be maintained for only about five minutes. On the other hand rates below 50% of maximum can be continued comfortably for many hours. Above about 60% of capacity the subjective demands of exercise escalate, endurance times tumble and fatigue can be expected to occur within an hour or so. Regular exercise does improve these aspects of performance and a trained man can tolerate higher relative work rates for longer than one who takes little exercise. In fact experienced mountaineers, polar travellers and workers such as lumberjacks appear to operate all day at rates corresponding to about 60% of their maximum oxygen intakes but rarely work harder than this. This accounts at least partially for the wide range of performance found amongst people hill walking, especially the inexperienced, since a given speed may require a comfortable 40% from one with a high working capacity but a hard 60% from another less well endowed. In practice it means that any physical activity expected to last for most of the day should not exceed 40–50% of the individual's maximum oxygen intake, if fatigue is to be avoided. (50% of maximum oxygen intake is attained at a pulse rate during exercise of about 130 beats/min). In the fatigued state the reduced level of performance may be limited to 20–30% of the individual's maximum and amount to a practical incapacity in some situations.

The effect of terrain on the energy cost of walking

Walking on the road and other hard smooth surfaces at 3–4 mph demands 30–40% of the average person's working capacity and can be maintained comfortably for many hours. This basic energy cost of progression may be affected by heavy protective clothing and footwear and a load of 50–60 lbs increases it by about one third. However, the economy of walking is very sensitive to any alteration in the normal swinging gait, and it is on this that different conditions under-foot have their effect. Terrain may do this in two ways, either by requiring a greater lift of the feet or by shortening the effective length of the stride. Of the first, rough stony ground, long grass and heather and deep soft snow are typical and the second, sliding surfaces such as loose snow or sand. Surfaces commonly found on hills and moorland may increase demands by up to 50% whilst loose sand and soft snow may double the energy cost of walking at usual speeds. Horizontal speeds may have to be halved to keep the energy demands within tolerable limits. On gentle gradients the nature of the surface has important effects on the energy cost of ascending or descending since the horizontal component of progression contributes significantly to the total energy cost. However, on slopes greater than about 1 in 5 the surface has little influence since the energy demands now arise almost entirely from the vertical movement of the climber and his load. For the average person, rates of ascent of 1500—2000 ft per hour correspond to about 50% of capacity. On descending similar gradients the energy cost of vertical movement is about 1/5th that of ascending and descents of 3000 ft per hour are the equivalent of 3½ — 4 mph on the level. Indeed, it is likely to be leg strength and technique rather than energy production that limit rates of descent. When descending much of the potential energy is absorbed by the muscles acting as brakes and reappears as heat, so that despite a relatively low energy production one becomes extremely warm.

Generally, at low altitudes a satisfactory rate of progress can be achieved with tolerable work rates. However, at altitudes exceeding about 10,000 ft the lower oxygen pressure significantly reduces the working capacity and this combined with difficult terrain may make it necessary to work close to maximum in order to make acceptable progress. Frequent rest pauses are required and both endurance and daily achievements suffer accordingly. Energy demands may not be the sole factors involved in fatigue during hill and mountain walking, and stature and physical strength may also influence the relative effects of terrain so that, for example, conditions possible to adults may be extremely hard for younger people.

The Nature of Exposure Accidents

In a review of 23 incidents of accidental hypothermia (exposure) in British hills in which 25 people died, Pugh, in 1966, identified walking to the point of exhaustion, wet clothing and mental impairment as the principal factors common to each incident. They invariably occurred within five or six hours of setting out and in conditions of high winds, temperatures near freezing, and precipitation.

Bad weather, fatigue and exposure

The physical stresses imposed by bad weather arise from two sources of increased demands on energy output. These are the direct mechanical effects of high winds and the more complex requirement of maintaining body heat.

Strong head winds exert horizontal forces, that the walker must overcome, in addition to the demand made by surfaces and speed. Similarly cross winds must be resisted, with consequent decreases in efficiency. At normal walking speeds a head wind corresponding to a fresh breeze (force 5) increases oxygen intake by one third whilst a gale (force 6–8) doubles it. Inevitably speed will be affected, and in a gale, one working at a rate within 50% of his capacity may be reduced to about 1½ mph. In practical terms high winds, especially head winds might halve the speed of travel expected on a calmer day and the length of excursions on windy days need to be planned accordingly.

The second aspect of the weather and its effect on energy output is concerned with the threat it poses to the maintenance of the body's heat. The cooling power of the environment is greatly increased by winds, an effect which can be adequately resisted only by rather sophisticated clothing. Thermal appreciation of the environment and the physiological responses to it are affected by a combination of the temperatures of the skin and the centre of the body (core temperature). The skin temperature is almost entirely dependent on the environment whilst the core temperature is related to energy production and rises during activity. Generally, the environment is modified by the use of clothing (adjustments) to obtain a narrow range of comfortable temperatures in the microclimate close to the skin, over a wide range of environmental temperatures. Thus on a cold day an inactive person who feels cold, can improve his comfort either by increasing his clothing and so raising his skin temperature or failing that he must increase his activity when the rise in his core temperature will allow him to tolerate his low skin temperature. Similarly if a man working hard feels warm he removes clothing which lowers his skin temperature and he feels cooler although his core temperature remains high.

The initial stages of an exposure accident are concerned with loss of clothing protection. The thermal insulation of ordinary clothing assemblies is at least halved by winds and movement. When clothing is also wet its insulation becomes negligible, and indeed, the wearer may be effectively nude since the temperature of the clothing next to his skin may be reduced to that of the ambient wet bulb.

In the face of the failure of his clothing the exposure victim attempts to balance his heat loss and improve his comfort by increased activity. If excessive cooling continues the low skin temperature initiates a reflex physiological increase in heat output, produced by an involuntary increase in muscle tension or activity overtly apparent in shivering. Here the muscles act purely as heat engines and perform no mechanical work. This involuntary heat production may increase oxygen consumption by as much as 20% of the maximum uptake. Not only does it occur during inactivity but also to the same degree during activity when it summates with the current mechanical oxygen requirement. In severe conditions a person already working voluntarily at a rate requiring 50% of his maximum oxygen intake may also have an involuntary oxygen intake amounting to 20% so that he is in fact using oxygen at 70% of his capacity and is therefore under considerable stress. Extremely fit people may be able to cope with such high energy production, but those with low working capacities may be overstressed, become fatigued, unable to maintain an adequate heat output and presently succumb to hypothermia. In fact, no man is immune to exposure if his clothing is ineffective because even with high energy outputs low skin temperatures will persist and muscle cooling and a gradual decline in central body temperature will result. This is particularly likely to occur in thin individuals. Muscle cooling results in weakness and loss of co-ordination and a reduction in both voluntary and involuntary heat production so that a spiral of failure to maintain body heat precipitates the exposure victim into hypothermia unless he obtains shelter. The extreme discomfort and misery associated with low skin temperatures has an appalling effect on morale and may well be partially responsible for the failure to make sensible decisions that is often associated with exposure accidents.

Below a certain body temperature (about 34°C) the involuntary thermogenesis fails and the body then cools passively under the physical influences of the environment. Continuing to travel merely increases the exposure and hastens the onset of collapse. The situation can only be reversed by preventing further heat loss allowing the body to rewarm. The insulation of even wet clothing is significantly improved by shelter, reduction in movement and the prevention of further evaporative heat loss.

Practical application for safety in hill walking

Generally speaking hill and mountain walking in the British Isles is a pleasurable and beneficial recreation within the capabilities of most healthy people without any special physical training. Nonetheless, mountain activities can be arduous especially for those with low working capacities and a poor history of physical activity. Such persons may easily be unhappily extended by over-enthusiastic or domineering leadership, and in any case possess a poor reserve in the face of deteriorating conditions. For optimal enjoyment and safety people undertaking cross country hikes should be able to proceed at a pace comfortably within their personal limitations. Groups, where possible, should be composed of individuals of similar physical ability and the length of their excursions planned accordingly. In any case the pace of a party should be set by the slowest members who may otherwise have to work at too high a proportion of their capacities in order to match the speed of the stronger walkers.

With regard to the weather — strong winds greatly increase the effort of walking and practical safe ranges may be halved. It is of interest that exposure and fatigue accidents rarely occur in polar regions where travelling is prohibited by drift at wind speeds exceeding about 12 knots (force 4—5). Stormy conditions should be considered as being immediately dangerous. Efficient wind and waterproof clothing will greatly reduce the likelihood of exposure, but the demands of battling against high winds makes it extremely unwise to travel under these conditions. When caught out by bad weather it is almost always safest to take adequate shelter — which should be carried by the walker — well before the point of exhaustion, and when the body's protective heat producing mechanisms are still intact.

Outdoor recreation should challenge the individual's self sufficiency rather than face him with a formidable task with which he personally may not be physically capable of coping.

FURTHER READING

Physical exercise and fatigue

Ästrand, P-O, and Rodahl, K. Text book of work physiology. *McGraw-Hill, 1970.*

Gleser, M.A., & Vogel, J.A. (1973). Endurance capacity for prolonged exercise on bicycle ergometer. *J. appl. Physiol. 34* (4). 438–442.

Effects of terrain on the energy cost of walking

Durnin, J.V.G.A. (1955). Oxygen consumption, energy expenditure and efficiency of climbing with loads at low altitudes. *J. Physiol. 128,* 294–309.

Pugh, L.G.C.E. (1958). Muscular exercise on Mount Everest. *J. Physiol. 141,* 233–261.

Soule, R.G., & Goldman, R.F. (1972). Terrain coefficients for energy cost prediction, *J. appl. Physiol. 32.* (5), 706–708.

Davies, C.T.M., & Barnes, C. (1972). Negative (eccentric) work. II. Physiological responses to walking uphill and downhill on a motor driven treadmill. *Ergonomics, 15* (2) 121–131.

Effects of weather and exposure

Pugh, L.G.C.E. (1966a). Accidental hypothermia in walkers, climbers and campers: Report to the Medical Commission on Accident Prevention. *Brit. med. J. i,* pp 123–129.

Pugh, L.G.C.E. (1966b). Clothing insulation and accidental hypothermia in youth. *Nature, 209,* 5030, pp 1281–1285, March 26, 1966.

Pugh, L.G.C.E. (1971). The influence of wind resistance in running and walking and the mechanical efficiency of work against horizontal or vertical forces. *J. physiol. 213,* pp 255–276.

Pugh, L.G.C.E. (1972). Accidental hypothermia among hill walkers and climbers in Britain. In: Environmental effects on work performance. Edit: G. R. Cumming, A. W. Taylor, D. Snidal. *Canadian Association of Sports Sciences, Congress on Sports Medicine,* July 1967.

Discussion

Sir Jack Longland. What is the physiological difference between a fell-runner and a high mountain climber?

Dr. Edwards. Training for running is very specific in its effects. The cross country runner has a large heart and very well adapted running muscles. He is at risk as a mountaineer however. Bonington for instance will have a lower peak fitness but a greater all-round ability.

Dr. Brotherhood. I am a runner. Yesterday at lunch-time I ran up Moel Siabod, with a climber, and he ended up a long way behind. Last night we did the Snowdon Horseshoe together and I was much more tired than he. He made the pace. That was a very nice demonstration of the point.

Mr. Waller. Can a man be calibrated so as to assess his work output?

Dr. Edwards. Yes.

Expedition Travel and Your Health

PETER STEELE

Preparations

Besides your travel documents do not forget to take with you:—
— Form E III or your medical insurance policy (see later).
— Medicines with which you are already being treated. The dosage and pharmac-
  ological name should be written on the bottle since proprietary names vary in
  different countries.
— Special medical information which can be imprinted on a bracelet or medallion
  i.e. blood group, drug allergy, diabetic or steroid treatment dosage. This is
  safer than a card carried in the pocket and may be lifesaving in an emergency.
— Spare spectacles or your lens prescription.
— Whistle (for girls), in case bottom-pinching gets out of hand. Remember, in
  many countries long hair = hippie, and undeserved rough handling may be
  given by the police. In some holiday resorts cheap drugs are sold which may
  be impure and dangerous; the penalties abroad for trafficking are just as
  severe as at home. V.D. is never caught from cracked cups or lavatory seats.
— Medical kit (see below) and booklet.

Medical checks: A chest X-ray before will allow comparison later in case you
contact Tuberculosis, which is still wide-spread in some under-developed countries.
Tooth fillings tend to loosen in cold so a dental check-up may save you agony
later. Suffer the indignity of an examination for piles if you suspect them. Feet
should be in good shape as much will be expected of them.

INSURANCE

Falling ill abroad can be very expensive. The European Economic Community
(EEC) Belgium, Denmark, France, West Germany, Ireland, Italy, Luxembourg
and the Netherlands, have reciprocal arrangements with our own National Health
Service. The detailed workings of the scheme are laid out in Form SA.28, issued
by the Department of Health and Social Security. This explains how the

118

certificate of entitlement to medical treatment (Form E III) may be obtained. It is not available to self-employed or unemployed persons.

Similar arrangements for free medical care exist in Bulgaria, Poland, Norway, Sweden and Yugoslavia. When in doubt the embassies of these countries should be consulted for details.

Elsewhere the cost of consultation, medicines, treatment and hospital care must be paid for by the patient. As this could be financially crippling, full health insurance is a wise precaution. You should consult a reputable company for advice on the policies available. A 'package deal' insurance includes baggage, personal accident and medical expenses up to £1000, two weeks cover costing about £2. A separate medical policy has a £2 minimum charge so has no advantage. The comprehensive insurances put out by the AA and RAC cover medical expenses. Routine dental treatment is not usually included in the policy.

Insurance covers the cost of medical treatment abroad or of flying the sick person home — this may be safest and cheapest in the long run.

Don't forget to insure every member of the party.

If you incur medical expenses, present your policy to the doctor and ask him to send the bill direct to your insurance company; if you pay cash, keep a receipt which will be honoured on your return.

If you are going to take part in "high-risk sports" you will need a more specific insurance cover. You should consult a company who specialise in this field and will give you an individual quote.

Immunization can protect you from certain infectious diseases that are common in countries abroad but rare at home. Your local District Community Physician's Department will advise you on the innoculation necessary for a particular country you may wish to visit and how to obtain them, either at a clinic or through your family doctor. Do not leave it to the last moment as a full course can take up to three months to complete properly.

Immunization is not obligatory in Europe or North America, but it is wise to be protected against:—

(i) Typhoid, Paratyphoid A & B and Tetanus (TABT). Two injections are given one month apart. An unpleasant reaction, with a sore arm and headache is not uncommon and you must avoid alcohol for 24 hours. After a wound from a dirty object or an animal bite you should obtain a booster dose of Tetanus Toxoid.

(ii) Smallpox, Yellow Fever and Cholera. Although not obligatory for Europe, it is wise to keep up to date. Smallpox immunization is compulsory for Asia, Australia and parts of Africa; Yellow Fever for Central and South America and Central Africa. A valid International Certificate must be carried. Smallpox immunity lasts three years and Yellow Fever ten years. Cholera immunization will soon no longer be compulsory. It may partly protect the individual for a short period but its value in international control of the disease is in doubt.

(iii) Diphtheria, Poliomyelitis and Tuberculosis (B.C.G.). Immunization is given to most children and lasts, so usually need not be repeated.

Three months should be allowed for a full course of immunization, but in emergency a 'crash course' of Smallpox, TABT, Yellow Fever (and Cholera) can be given in 15 days.

(iv) Malaria is not a danger in Europe, North America and the near East; but if you visit a malarial zone elsewhere in the world, a course of prophylactic anti-malarial drugs should be prescribed by your doctor starting one week before departure and continuing for at least a month after return.

Human Gamma Globulin has gained the reputation as a universal protector, especially against infective hepatitis (jaundice).

The following advice aims to help you avoid the illnesses commonly met abroad, most of which can be treated by yourself in the first instance. If, however, the condition rapidly worsens or does not improve within 24–48 hours you should consult a doctor. Several different drugs can be used to treat any one illness; those recommended here are included in the suggested medical kit at the end of the booklet. Approved names of drugs are generally used; proprietary preparations have inverted commas. Unless stated differently a medicine should be taken four times a day. Children's doses are usually half the adult dose.

A. Traveller's Diarrhoea

Gippy Tummy, Delhi Belly, Kathmandu Quickstep — it has as many names as patent remedies and strikes most travellers at some stage in their journey making more trouble than all the other illnesses mentioned here, put together. The causes are usually untraceable but may include gluttony, change in climate and an upset in the bacteria that are normal and necessary in the bowel. Infection with disease-causing organisms carried in water and food is less common.

Much of the pleasure of travelling abroad comes from eating local food and drinking wine. Be moderate to prevent the tummy upset that will spoil your holiday, and even make you into a useless member of the party.

Precautions:

(a) Water warrants the utmost care as carelessness may be very costly. In some clean hotels and restaurants the water is safe to drink. Stream and river water is likely to be polluted unless it comes directly from a hillside spring, and glacial mud or mica in alpine rivers is especially irritant to the gut. If you are in doubt drinking water should be sterilized.

— Boiling briskly for a few seconds kills most organisms (including amoeba cysts and infectious hepatitis virus). So drink tea or coffee.

— Water-purifying tablets. Chemical treatment is less effective than boiling, takes longer and leaves a taste of chlorine, but is useful if boiling is not practicable.

— Filters purify water less surely than boiling, but they do get rid of the murky colour of suspended organic matter.

(b) Drinks. Bottled fizz is usually safe. Wine and spirits drunk in moderation are harmless, but mixing them with water has no 'sterilizing action'.

(c) Food. Freshly and thoroughly cooked food is safe since any bacteria will have been killed by the heat. So avoid pre-cooked and handled foods, especially when flies abound. Peel fruit and vegetables; thorough washing is only second best so beware of salads, lettuces and watercress. Keep to well-advertised brands of ice-cream, and risk shellfish only if you have a tough stomach.

(d) Hygiene. Toilets abroad are often dirty; you may have to squat and keep your balance by holding on to the walls. So wash your hands carefully with soap as soon as possible afterwards. Take your own toilet paper as newsprint is rough and fragile. At campsites dig a latrine hole well away from the tents, and your water supply.

Brush your teeth in clean water only — chewing gum is a useful temporary cleaner.

N.B. *CHOLERA.* 1973 saw a worldwide epidemic notably in parts of Italy. The Cholera organisms come only from the human intestine and are spread by faecally contaminated water, not by direct contact or inhalation. Raw shellfish collect the bugs so are particularly dangerous. A sudden onset of profuse watery diarrhoea in a known epidemic area calls for immediate attention.

Treatment of Traveller's Diarrhoea

The illness usually clears up on its own in 2—3 days. You may also vomit and because a lot of body water is lost you may feel groggy. Go to bed and drink unlimited fluids (at least a pint an hour). Avoid eating — except dried toast and peeled grated apple gone brown (pectin). A binding medicine will speed recovery. A dose of the 'Everest Blunderbuss Cocktail' constipates most people for a week: Kaolin powder 2 tablespoons, Tincture of morphine (chlorodyne) 4—6 drops, Codeine phosphate 30mg., and 'Lomotil' 4—6 tabs. or any of these singly if all are not available. Antibiotics, though fashionable, should not be used blindly since they kill normal bacteria, which are protective, as well as poison-producing ones.

Dysentery

If diarrhoea does not stop within 24 hours on this treatment, or if blood appears in the stools, a doctor should be consulted since you may be suffering from dysentery. If you cannot find help the best drug to start with is Co-trimoxazole ('Septrin', 'Bactrim'). Bacillary Dysentery starts suddenly with acute diarrhoea, fever and malaise. Amoebic Dysentery causes slimy mucus and blood and warrants laboratory investigation and treatment. Its severity builds up slowly over several days.

Worms

Worms are common in tropical countries. They cause an itchy bottom and can often be seen in the stools. Take a Piperazine ('Pripsen') sachet.

Indigestion

Magnesium Trisilicate gets rid of wind and may even help a hangover.

Constipation

Drink plenty and eat fruit; if this fails take two laxative tablets ('Senokot').

N.B. Beware the person who feels sick, has no appetite, a dirty, coated tongue and pain in the belly. If the abdomen is tender, particularly in the right lower quarter, you should suspect appendicitis and visit a doctor.

Waterworks

Infection is more common in women. It begins as frequent passing of urine with burning pain. Drink a pint of water hourly with a tablespoon of bicarbonate of soda and take an antibiotic if it does not improve in a day.

B. Infection

General infections

Antibiotics must not be eaten indiscriminately but if you develop an infection with a high fever and rapid pulse when you are away in the wilds on your own, blind therapy with a broad spectrum bug-killing drug may be justified. Co-trimoxazole ('Septrin', 'Bactrim') or Amoxycillin ('Amoxyl') should be taken for a full five day course.

Local infections

Eyes. If the eyes are pink and feel gritty wear dark glasses and put in 'Brolene' ointment. A few drops of Amethocaine will anaesthetise the cornea to let you dig out a foreign body. Homatropine dilates the pupil and relieves painful spasm but will temporarily blur the vision.

Ears. Keep dry with a light plug of cotton wool but don't poke matches in. If there is discharge and pain an antibiotic may be needed.

Sinusitis gives a headache (felt worse on stooping), 'toothache' in the upper jaw, and often a thick discharge from the nose. Inhale steam with Tinct. Benz. or sniff the tea brew with a towel over your head to help drainage. Decongestant drops may clear the nose if it is mildly bunged up, but true sinusitis may need an antibiotic.

Throat. Cold dry air irritates the throat and makes it sore. Gargle with a couple of Aspirin or table salt dissolved in warm water; or suck antiseptic lozenges.

Teeth. When brushing teeth is difficult, chewing gum is useful. If a filling comes out a plug of cotton wool soaked in oil of cloves eases the pain; gutta percha, softened in boiling water is easily plastered into the hole as a temporary filling. Hot salt mouthwashes encourage pus to discharge from a dental abscess but an antibiotic will be needed.

Feet take a hammering, so boots must fit and be comfortable. Climbing boots are rarely necessary on the approach march to a mountain; gym shoes or flip-flops are useful. At the first sign of rubbing put on a plaster.

BLISTERS: Burst with a sterile blade or needle (boiled for three minutes or held in a flame until red hot). Remove dead skin, spray with Tinct. Benz. and cover the raw area with zinc oxide plaster; leave it in place for several days to allow new skin to form.

ATHLETES FOOT: Wash with soap and dry carefully between the toes; then dust with antifungal powder ('Tineafax') and wear open sandals.

MUSCLE ACHE: Rub Methyl Salicylate (Wintergreen) ointment deeply.

CRAMPS: Take extra salt in your diet or use salt tablets. Modify exercise until you are fit.

C. Sun

The sun may be a stealthy enemy. Sunlight reflects strongly off snow and light-coloured rocks; its rays can penetrate hazy cloud and are more powerful the higher you climb. Until you have a good tan protect yourself with clothing and a hat. An ultraviolet barrier cream ('Uvistat') screens the skin but with excessive sun it merely acts as fat in the frying process. Rationing sunlight is cheaper and more effective.

Sunburn: Calamine soothes shrimp-pink prickly hot skin; if you turn bright lobster and blister you are severely burnt and should obtain a steroid cream.

Sunstroke: If you develop a high temperature and feel ill after being in strong sun, cool yourself with cold water sponging or ice packs, drink ample fluid and take Aspirin to lower your temperature and relieve headache. Collapse from sunstroke warrants urgent medical help.

Snowblindness is caused by an ultraviolet burn of the cornea, resulting in intense pain and swelling of the eyes. It can be prevented by wearing dark glasses or goggles; horizontal slits cut in a piece of cardboard will do in emergency. Amethocaine drops will ease the pain enough to reach camp. Then put Homatropine drops and 'Brolene' ointment in the eyes and wear dark glasses or cover with eye-pads and a bandage if the pain is severe.

D. Travel Sickness

If you know you are prone to suffer take one anti-histamine tablet (Promethazine, 'Phenergan' 25 mg.) before the journey and one more if sickness continues. A long and tedious journey will pass in a soporific daze so do not drive. Chlorpheniramine, 'Piriton' 4 mg. may be used instead if you have to keep alert.

E. Nature's Annoyances

From flies and mosquitos, bees, wasps, ants and hornets; from fleas, lice and bedbugs; from sea urchins and jellyfish; and from a host of other creepy-crawlies we pray deliverance. Repellant sprays (containing Dimethylphthalate) only last a few hours; DDT may repel a few. If you are unfortunate enough to be attacked the basic problem is itching. If there is a sting remove it. Treat the pain and irritation with Calamine cream or lotion, and Promethazine or Chlorpheniramine tablets. Scratching with grubby finger nails may cause the bit to go septic.

Arthropods: Lice, fleas and bedbugs are common in huts; 'Lorexane' helps to keep them at bay.

Mosquitos are usually only a bother at lower altitudes. A net makes sleeping more comfortable but does not guarantee protection from malaria.

Snakes. Clean the area and suck the wound. Do *not* slash the skin with razor blades or urinate on it. Remember only poisonous snakes cause snakebite poisoning – it is quite rare. Local hospitals probably carry the antiserum against the common local snakes.

Dogs. Bites always warrant an anti-tetanus booster. Rabies is rare but possible.

Leeches are most troublesome during and shortly after the monsoon in the tropics. You do not feel them and may only notice a bootful of blood at the end of the day. Open sandals let you see them early – a lighted cigarette or salt makes the leech drop off, and insect repellant keeps them at bay.

Wasp stings – vinegar. *Bee stings* – bicarbonate of soda.

Bilharzia is widespread in parts of Africa so avoid tempting cool-offs in slow flowing rivers and lakes where the flukes breed.

Poisoning. Try to make the person sick by drinking a salt solution or sticking the fingers down his throat.

F. Injury

Nature is a wonderful healer if given adequate encouragement.

Cuts and grazes go septic quickly so must be taken seriously. Wash thoroughly with soap and water or an antiseptic solution (gentian violet or potassium permanganate). Cover with a sterile plaster strip or non-stick ('Melolin') gauze. Antiseptic cream may be used if the wound is difficult to clean adequately, but it tends to make the dressing stick and keeps the wound moist, which delays healing. Anchor dressings are useful for awkward places, i.e. fingers, heels. If the cut is clean and gaping bring the edges together with 'Steristrips' in place of stitches.

Deep Wounds. Firm pressure on a No. 15 wound dressing will stop most bleeding. If blood seeps through put more dressing on top, secure with absorbent crepe bandage, and keep up the pressure, elevating the part if possible.

Burns when superficial are simply skin wounds. Leave open to the air to form a dry crust under which healing goes on. If this is not possible cover with

'Melolin' dressings. Burn creams offer no magic. Deep burns must be kept scrupulously clean and treated urgently by a doctor. Give drinks freely to replace lost fluid.

Sprains. Apply a firm crepe or elastoplast bandage. If painful movement and swelling persist, suspect a fracture. Cold compresses help reduce swelling.

Fractures: Immobilize the part by splinting to a rigid structure; the arm can be strapped to the chest, both legs can be tied together. Temporary splints can be made from a rolled newspaper, an ice-axe or a branch. Pain may be agonizing and is due to movement of broken bone ends on each other.

Pain

Pain-killers fall into three strengths for different grades of pain:
mild — Aspirin (lowers the temperature but can irritate the stomach). Paracetamol is a useful alternative.
moderate — Pentazocine 'Fortral' (can cause hallucinations).
severe — Pethidine, Morphine (may depress the breathing dangerously. Only available on special prescription).

Unconsciousness

The causes range from drowning to head injury, diabetes to epilepsy. Untrained laymen should only attempt to place the victim in 'the draining position' — lying on his side with the head lower than the chest to allow secretions, blood or vomit to drain away from the lungs. Hold the chin forward to prevent the tongue falling back and obstructing the airway. Don't try any fancy manoeuvres unless you are practised, as you may do more harm than good.

Fainting

Lie down and raise the legs to return extra blood to the brain.

G. Exposure

Mountain Hypothermia occurs when the temperature of the central core of the body falls below about 35°C owing to the combined effect of wind, wet and cold. Exhaustion and low morale worsen it. If someone behaves in an uncharacteristic manner — apathetic, stumbling, swearing, uncontrolled shivering — be on your guard. He may suddenly collapse and die.
    Stop and shelter the victim i.e. tent, polythene bag, lean-to. Re-warm him by

skin-to-skin contact. Dress him in dry spare clothes and put him in a sleeping bag. Give hot drinks and a nip of alcohol can do no harm and may give him the boost he needs to get down by himself after he is rested and rewarmed. If his condition does not improve you will have to call help to evacuate him by stretcher.

When at base he should be slowly rewarmed in a water bath at 42–44°C, though some would recommend higher initial water temperatures, up to 50°C.

H. High Altitude Ills

Up to 12,000 ft. you have little to fear — no more than on an ordinary mountain walking holiday. If you are not shaping up too well reconsider the wisdom of climbing any higher for you are entering the realm of the high, thin, cold, dry air. Slow ascent is the secret of easy acclimatization to altitude. Breathing and heartbeat speed up, a thumping headache and nausea make you feel miserable. At night sleep is elusive ('Mogadon' 1 tab.). You may notice a peculiar irregularity in the pattern of breathing (Cheyne Stokes respiration) when, for a short period, breathing appears to have stopped and then gradually increases in stepwise fashion until it eventually falls off again. The normal output of urine may be diminished and very dilute.

The unpleasant symptoms of acclimatization usually pass off in a few days, but they may develop into Acute Mountain Sickness. This rarely starts below 15,000 ft. so is unlikely in the Alps but may occur in Africa, the Andes or Himalayas.

If you begin to feel more ill than you would expect for your own degree of fitness and acclimatization, go down quickly and stay down. Acute Mountain Sickness can quickly develop into High Altitude Pulmonary (lung) Oedema, or Cerebral (brain) Oedema, i.e. swelling due to abnormal retention of water. Women are more susceptible in the days before their periods. This is a potentially lethal disease the cause of which is not understood, but it can affect all ages, the fit and the unfit, those who have risen quickly and those who have not.

If someone suddenly feels, and looks, puffy in the face, goes blue round the lips, has bubbly breathing and even pink frothy sputum, evacuate them urgently to a lower altitude. Oxygen (if available) and a diuretic drug Frusemide ('Lasix') may help to clear water from the lungs; but they are no substitute for rapid descent which has a miraculous effect. Those who have suffered once are likely to do so again, so must beware.

Thrombosis. Persistent deep calf tenderness and a slight fever and pain — more than a muscular ache — may indicate a vein thrombosis. Women on The Pill are especially at risk. You should rest, preferably with the legs bandaged and elevated, and start an antibiotic. This is a serious illness so descend and seek medical advice.

Piles commonly trouble people at high altitude, probably due to raising the pressure inside the abdomen by overbreathing while carrying heavy loads. A haemorrhoidal suppository ('Anusol') gives temporary relief.

Dry cough is eased by inhaling steam. Codeine Phosphate 15 mg. dampens it. In a violent bout of coughing you can fracture a rib; the agony may make you think you have had a heart attack but the chances of this are slim.

Frostbite should not occur if you are clothed properly and take commonsense precautions. If you get very cold, rewarm the part quickly against warm flesh (someone else's if possible). Do *not* rub it or you will damage the skin and cause further wounding which may become infected.

Drugs which dilate the blood vessels (Vasodilators) have no specific action against frostbite although they make you feel a warm glow inside. This can be very dangerous as you are losing heat from the rest of your body and you may be tipped into Exposure.

If a foot is frozen it is better to walk on it back to a low camp where you can rapidly rewarm it in water 42–44°C. Thereafter the victim must be carried.

Women. When travelling or climbing your periods may stop temporarily; this is nothing to worry about. Women on the Pill are most at risk from thrombosis, cystitis and thrush.

Medical Equipment

A prescription is needed for several items. You should ask your doctor to sign the entire list as a private prescription (i.e. it has to be paid for, as medical equipment to be taken abroad is not available on the N.H.S.).

(a) LEADER'S KIT (for 4–6 persons for 2 months)

Basic

Dressings	1	Plaster Dressing Strip 36"
	4	Anchor Dressings
	1	Zinc Oxide Plaster 1" x 5m
	1	Elastoplast 3" x 5m
	1	Steristrip (¼" x 4")
	1	Bandage Crepe 3"
	1	" Cotton 2"
	1	" Triangular
	4	Gauze Squares Plain

	4	Gauze Squares Melolin 4" x 4"
	4	" Melolin 2" x 2"
	2	" Jelonet 4" x 4"
	1	Cotton Wool compressed
	1	Wound Dressing No. 15
	1	Netelast (F) Head Dressing
Cleaning	1	Soap bar
		Gentian Violet (crystals)
	1	Brolene Antiseptic eye ointment
Instruments	1	Scissors blunt/sharp
	1	Forceps oblique end
	1	Scalpel blade (sterile)
	4	Safety pins
	2	Luggage labels
	1	Marker pencil

Medicines

Pain-killers (mild)	60	Aspirin
" (mod)	20	Pentazocine (Fortral)
(severe)	10	Pethidine 50 mg tab
Antibiotic	40	Co-Trimoxazole (Septrin, Bactrim)
Antihistamine	40	Promethazine (Phenergan) 25 mg
	20	Chlorpheniramine (Piriton) 4 mg
Sleeping	20	Nitrazepam (Mogadon)
	100	Water Purifying tabs
Diarrhoea	½lb	Kaolin powder
(and cough)	40	Codeine Phosphate 15 mg
	40	Diphenoxylate (Lomotil)
Constipation	10	Senokot
Indigestion	30	Magnesium Trisilicate
Salt	20	Salt tablets
Vitamins	40	Multivite
	40	Vit. C
Anti-worm	4 sach	Piperazine ('Pripsen')
Eyes/Ears	1	Brolene 4G
Eyes	1	Amethocaine drops
	2	Homatropine drops
	2	Fluorescein papers

Nose	1	Otrivin Antistin spray
Throat	40	Hibitane lozenges
		Gentian Violet crystals
Teeth		Oil of Cloves
	1	gutta percha temporary filling
Skin		
Sun creams	1	Uvistat
Lips	1	Lipsyl
Insect Repellant	1	Flypel
Etc.	1	Calamine cream
	1	Methyl Salicylate & Iodex ointment
	25	Tinct Benzoin
	1 tin	Tineafax powder (25G)
	10	Anusol suppositories
	1	Lorexane DDT powder
Diuretic	20	Frusemide (Lasix) 40 mg
Stimulant	4	Amphetamine (Dexedrine)

(b) INDIVIDUAL KIT

Dressings	1	Plaster strip 12" x 2½"
	1	Zinc oxide 1" x 3m
	4	Melolin 2" x 2"
	1	Crepe Bandage 3"
	1	Razor Blade
	1	Luggage label
	1	Marker pencil
	10	Fortral
	20	Phenergan (25mg)
Diarrhoea	20	Codeine Phosphate
Sun	1 tube	Uvistat
	1	Lipsyl
Throat	40	Hibitane lozenges
Skin/eyes/Ears	1	Brolene (4G)
	100	Water Purifying tablets

Discussion

Dr. Rennie. (1) The worst thing you can do is to take off your goggles in a white-out.

(2) A doctor on an Expedition who does not know what to do about high altitude illness is worse than no doctor at all.

(3) Train your Sherpas to cook properly.

Dr. Steele. Agreed there is no point in having an expedition doctor unless he is *properly* trained.

Dr. Clarke. The cost of the 1975 British Everest Expedition's Suncream quoted to me has ben £350. I feel simpler things work just as well. I use my daughter's nappy cream.

Dr. Steele. There was an article in WHICH about three years ago. All sun creams are just screens. It is cheaper to wear a hat or shirt. Nestle's condensed milk does the job just as well.

Dr. Houston. Much diarrhoea is caused by drinking water which has been boiled but which has mica in it.

Anon. As to water — if you can see the origin of your stream — as you sometimes can — use its water without purifying.

Dr. Steele drew attention to the slit goggles used by Eskimos and stated these could be made from cardboard in a few minutes if sun goggles were lost. Yak hair light filters had similarly been used.

There followed further lengthy discussion.

LIST OF PARTICIPANTS

J. T. H. ALLEN, BA, AKC, T. Cert.
15B Lawnsgreen Avenue,
Manchester, M21 2FH.

Executive Officer,
Young Explorers' Trust.
Alpine Club

S. ARMSTRONG, BSc., Cert. Ed.
Lagganlia Centre for Outdoor
Education, Kincraig, Kingussie,
Invernessshire.

Deputy Principal,
Lagganlia Centre for Outdoor
Education

M. F. BAKER
63 Gowan Avenue, London, SW6

Honorary Secretary,
Alpine Club

DR. G. BALLANCE, MB, BCh.
5 Sedley Taylor Road, Cambridge

Physician

L. BEER
School of Plant Biology,
University College of North Wales,
Bangor, Gwynedd.

Botanist

P. BELL
The Slack, Ambleside,
Cumbria, LA22 9DQ.

Engineer
Member of Mountain Rescue Team

LT. (MS) W. J. BLAKE
Institute of Naval Medicine,
Alverstoke, Gosport, Hants.

Royal Navy

P. BOARDMAN
29 Sandy Lane, Bramley, Cheshire.

Executive Officer,
British Mountaineering Council

DR. J. R. BROTHERHOOD, MB, BS.
4 Laycock Street, London, N.1.

Clinical Physiologist

132

WING COMMANDER D.G.P. BROWN, Royal Air Force
    MB, Ch.B.
    RAF Leuchars, Fife.

DR. C.R.A. CLARKE, MB, MRCP. Registrar in Neurology.
    6 Barnsbury Square, Alpine Club
    London, N1 1JL.

SQUADRON LEADER L.W. DAVIES, Warden, Outward Bound Mountain
    FRGS. School, Ullswater.
    Hederlanghals, Outward Bound Alpine Club
    Mountain School, Ullswater,
    Penrith, Cumbria.

DR. R.H.T. EDWARDS, Ph.D., MRCP. Physician; Co-Director Jerry Lewis
    1 Hood Avenue, Muscle Research Centre,
    East Sheen, SW14 7LH. Royal Postgraduate Medical School,
    London.

MAJOR J. W. FLEMING Alpine Club
    c/o School of Infantry,
    Warminster, Wilts.

LT. COL. H. FORBES, MB, BS, DPH. Royal Army Medical Corps
    Royal Army Medical College,
    Millbank, London, SW1.

SQUADRON LEADER J. W. GOADBY, Royal Air Force
    MRCS, LRCP, D. Obs., RCOG.
    Regional Medical Centre,
    RAF, Kinloss, Morayshire.

SURGEON COMMANDER F. GOLDEN, Royal Navy
    MB, BCH, D.Av. Med.
    R.N. Air Medical School,
    Seafield Park, Hillhead, Hants.

H. B. GREY Mountaineering Instructor
    Aberglaslyn Hall, Beddgelert,
    Gwynedd.

I.F.G. HAMPTON, B.Sc., Ph.D.
Dept. Physiology, The University,
Leeds, L52 9JT.

Physiologist

PROF. G.R. HERVEY, MA, MB, Ph.D.
Department of Physiology,
The University, Leeds, LS2 9JT.

Professor of Physiology.
Chairman: RNPRC
Survival-at-Sea Sub-Committee.

D. HOLSTEAD,
IM Marsh College of PE.,
Oakhill Road, Liverpool.

Head of Physiology Department

PROF. C. HOUSTON, MD.
88 Ledge Road, Burlington,
Vermont, USA.

Arctic Physiology
Programme of the Arctic
Institute of N. America.
Professor of Community Medicine,
University of Vermont.
Alpine Club.

DR. R. B. HUDDY, BM., BCh., MRCP.
Elm Bank, Garth Road, Marple,
Cheshire.

Consultant Physician.
Mountaineer

J. JACKSON
Plas-y-Brenin, Capel Curig, Gwynedd.

Principal, National Mountaineering
Centre. Alpine Club.

DR. F.S. JACKSON, FRCP.
Old Darras Hall, Ponteland,
Newcastle upon Tyne.

Consultant Cardiologist.
Alpine Club.

MRS. R. JAMES, MIAC.
Enlli, Lon y Ffrwd, Bangor,
Gwynedd.

Lecturer in Physical Education and
Outdoor Pursuits

R. JAMES
IM Marsh College of PE,
Oak Hill Road, Liverpool, L17 6BD.

Principal Lecturer in Outdoor
Education.
Alpine Club.

I.A.A. KELLAS, B.Sc.
6 Waterton Avenue, Mossley, Lancs.

Mountaineer

A. KNIBBS
Department of Physiology,
The University, Leeds.

Lecturer in Physical Education and
Exercise Physiology

A. J. LACK
Pindisports, 14 Holborn,
London, EC1.

Mountaineering Equipment Buyer

I.A. LEIGH
JSMTC, Fort George, Inverness

Principal, Joint Services Mountain
Training Committee

FL/LT R. LEITCH, MB, Ch.B.
10 Valetta Road, Thorney Island,
Emsworth, Hants.

Royal Air Force

DR. E. LEUTHOLT, MD.
Tödistrasse 36,
8002 Zurich.

Physician.
Swiss Foundation for Alpine Research

DR. E. LL. LLOYD, MB, Ch.B,
MRCP Ed, FFARCS,
The Royal Infirmary, Edinburgh,
EH3 9YW.

Senior Registrar in Anaesthetics

SIR JACK LONGLAND
Bridgeway, Bakewell,
Derbyshire, DE4 1DS.

Former President, B.M.C.
President, Alpine Club.

DR. CATHERINE MACINNES, MBBS.
Glenelg By Kyle, Highlands.

General Practitioner.
Mountain Rescue Team Leader.

DR. A.J.F. MACMILLAN,
RAF Institute of Aviation Medicine,
Farnborough, Hants.

Institute of Aviation Medicine.

W.D.MACPHERSON, OBE.
53 Albert Court,
Kensington Gore, London, SW7.

Alpine Club

MRS. W. D. MACPHERSON, MCSP.
53 Albert Court,
Kensington Gore, London, SW7.

Physiotherapist

DR. P. MARCUS, MD. DAvMed.　　　　Head of Cold Environment Research
　　Anvers, The Garth,　　　　　　　　Section, Institute of Aviation
　　Farnborough, Hants.　　　　　　　　Medicine.

MRS. J. MARCUS
　　Anvers, The Garth,
　　Farnborough, Hants.

BRIG. J. MARCHANT　　　　　　　　Commanding Officer,
　　Army Outward Bound School,　　　　Army Outward Bound School.
　　Tywyn, Merioneth.

DR. J.S. MILLEDGE, MD, MRCP Ed.　　Clinical Physiologist
　　114 Uxbridge Road,
　　Rickmansworth, Herts.

J. MILLS, MIAC.　　　　　　　　　　BMC Mountain Rescue Committee.
　　Llanrug Outdoor Activities Centre,
　　Llanrug, Caernarfon, Gwynedd.

PROFESSOR R. E. MOORE, MB, BS,　　Professor of Physiology,
　　Ph.D.　　　　　　　　　　　　　　Trinity College, Dublin.
　　Dept. of Physiology, Trinity College,
　　Dublin 2.

MRS. R. E. MOORE
　　Dept. of Physiology, Trinity College,
　　Dublin 2.

DR. J. D. NELMS, BSc., MBBS.　　　　Director, Army Personnel
　　Army Personnel Research　　　　　　Establishment.
　　Establishment,
　　c/o RAE Farnborough, Hants.

DR. A. GRAEME NICOL, MBCh.B.,　　Physician/Pathologist.
　　MRCP, Ph.D., MRC Path.　　　　　　Alpine Climbing Group.
　　14 Ballieswells Road, Bieldside,
　　Aberdeenshire.

PROF. N. E. ODELL　　　　　　　　　Professor of Geology.
　　Clare College, Cambridge.　　　　　　Alpine Club.

DR. J. D. OWEN
3, East Hill, Colchester,
CO12 QT, Essex.

General Practitioner

J. PAISLEY, DipEd,
Lagganlia Centre for Outdoor
Education, Kincraig, Kingussie.

Principal, Lagganlia Centre for
Outdoor Education.

DR. G.L.S. PAWAN, DSc, MRC Path,
FI. Biol., F.R.I.C.
Metabolic Div., Dept. of Medicine,
Middlesex Hospital, London, W.1.

Biochemist

DR. D. RENNIE, MD, MRCP,
1208 North Sheridan Road,
Lake Forest, Illinois 60045, USA.

Physician.
Mountaineer.

D. G. ROBERTSON, BSc.
8 Corringway, Crookham,
Aldershot, Hants.

Human Physiologist.
Member BMC Safety and Equipment
Committees

DR. B. ROSEDALE, MBBS, DCH,
DTM+H.
Thornsend, Kingsbury Hill,
Marlborough, Wilts.

General Practitioner.

H.B. SALES
1 Abbots Close, Guildford, GU2 5RW.

Alpine Club

B. SMITH, BA.
The Outdoor Centre, Nant B-H,
Trefriw, Gwynedd.

Mountaineer

DR. P. STANDING, MB, BS,
Withington Hospital, Manchester.

Mountaineer

P.R.C. STEELE, FRCS.
38 Canynge Square, Clifton,
Bristol, BS8 3LA.

Physician.
Author.
Alpine Club.

H. W. TILMAN
Bod-Owen, Nr. Barmouth, Gwynedd.

Explorer. Author.
Alpine Club.

DR. K.H.L. TODD   General Practitioner
    26 Rockwood Crescent,
    Woodhall Park, Pudsey, Yorks.

R. E. TWIGG, MIC,   Mountaineering Instructor.
    Llanrug Outdoor Activities Centre,
    Llanrug, Gwynedd.

I. WALLER   Outward Bound Trust.
    Middle Dodds, Crosthwaite,   Alpine Club
    Kendal, Cumbria, LA8 8HX.

M. P. WARD, MD, FRCS,   Consultant Surgeon.
    67 Woodsford Square,   Alpine Club.
    Addison Road, London, W.14.

DR. C. WARREN, FRCP, DCH,   Consultant Paediatrician.
    Buck Croft, Felsted, Essex.   Alpine Club.

MAJOR G. M. WARRICK,   Royal Engineers
    HQ UKLF, Salisbury, Wilts.

MRS. M. H. WESTMACOTT,   Alpine Club.
    26 Gordon Avenue, Stanmore,   Ladies Alpine Club.
    Middlesex.

PROF. E. S. WILLIAMS, MD, Ph.D.,   Professor of Nuclear
    M.R.C.P.,   Medicine, University of
    Bisney Cottage, Shamley Green,   London.
    Guildford, Surrey.   Alpine Club.

DR. W. R. WITHEY, Ph.D.,   Physiologist.
    RAF Institute of Aviation Medicine,
    Farnborough, Hants.

DR. J. WOLF, M.D.,   President of the Health
    Horolezecky Svaz Uv Cstv,   Committee of the
    Na Porici 12, 110 00 Praha,   Czechoslovak
    Czechoslovakia.   Mountaineering Union.

INDEX

NOTES

NOTES

NOTES